T009646

Healing
Your Past

Arian A. Sarris, LMFT

BALBOA.
PRESS

A DIVISION OF HAY HOUSE

ISBN: 978-1-4525-5065-7 (sc)
ISBN: 978-1-4525-5064-0 (e)

Library of Congress Control Number: 2012907225

Balboa Press books may be ordered through booksellers or by contacting:

Balboa Press
A Division of Hay House
1663 Liberty Drive
Bloomington, IN 47403
www.balboapress.com
1-(877) 407-4847

Because of the dynamic nature of the Internet, any web addresses or links contained in this book may have changed since publication and may no longer be valid. The views expressed in this work are solely those of the author and do not necessarily reflect the views of the publisher, and the publisher hereby disclaims any responsibility for them.

The author of this book does not dispense medical advice or prescribe the use of any technique as a form of treatment for physical, emotional, or medical problems without the advice of a physician, either directly or indirectly. The intent of the author is only to offer information of a general nature to help you in your quest for emotional and spiritual well-being. In the event you use any of the information in this book for yourself, which is your constitutional right, the author and the publisher assume no responsibility for your actions.

Any people depicted in stock imagery provided by Thinkstock are models, and such images are being used for illustrative purposes only.
Certain stock imagery © Thinkstock.

Printed in the United States of America

Balboa Press rev. date: 09/20/12

Contents

Introduction
Layers Of The Past

We are shaped by our childhood environment—our family beliefs, secrets, abuse, dysfunction. The person we become arises directly out of our survival choices. Not surprisingly, those survival patterns dominate our adult lives.

Besides our childhood, another layer of the past that controls us is past lives. Think of those deep issues that you struggled with for years. Even though you might find some relief and release through psychotherapy and counseling, they still persist.

I have found that, in guiding many of my clients into deeper levels of their inner work, they spontaneously go into past life situations. This gives us an opportunity to resolve issues at a soul level.

What is remarkable about past life work is that you can process as powerfully as if you are remembering your present-day childhood, and more importantly, you can begin to discover solutions to intractable problems, such as phobias, allergies, and disease.

When we feel helpless and overwhelmed by our patterns, it is hard to find a way out except by blaming others. *Healing Your Past* gives you another option for breaking through your internal logjam of blame to reach self-acceptance, and, ultimately, forgiveness of yourself and others. By using these techniques, you will be able to release the baggage you have been holding onto for lifetimes.

In this book you will find suggestions for dealing with specific situations and issues:

- Find ways to break free of the constraints of the past—both in your current and past lives.
- Discover new solutions to phobias, allergies, and seemingly-intractable personal issues.
- Use tools and exercises to create movement in your life.

- Move away from the victim/blame roles.
- Understand karmic issues as they manifest in your life, and take responsibility for healing them in past lives and now.
- Understand the larger purpose of disease, and work on freeing it from your life.
- Explore your Life Purpose and align yourself to your inner goals.

These non-traditional psychological and spiritual tools, such as visualization, past life work, metaphor, angel guides, and your Higher Self will help you heal your past and help you move forward into your future.

Isn't it time to stop being controlled by your past, and open to the possibility and joy of the present?

CHAPTER 1
CHANGE YOUR LIFE

Ask yourself the following questions: Does your life work? Are you happy? Have you forgiven your parents? Resolved your childhood issues? Or are you stuck in memories of abuse, anger, helplessness, abandonment? More importantly–do you tend to wallow around in those feelings and memories? Or are you ready to change your life? To get out of the rut you've been stuck in? To break out of the old way of thinking, acting, and believing? (How do you know you're even in that rut?)

I believe that within each of us there is an inexorable movement toward manifesting our Life Purpose, which is the reason we came onto this planet. Sometimes we discover it early in life, but most of us find it in our thirties and forties, after we've spent some time nibbling away at many our issues. (Carl Jung called it the "inward arc", when you started focusing on yourself instead of trying to be successful in the world.)

When you manifest your Life Purpose, it feels like everything has fallen into place; and conversely, when you are not fulfilling it, you feel discontented, frustrated, and unhappy. Your soul wants you to function at your maximum capability. Yet a 100 percent commitment to your work (whether it is your external job or internal evolution) may be difficult because a major part of your energy is locked away in old patterns, beliefs, fears, and addictions.

The extent to which you are governed by these experiences and fears indicates the level of control the baggage of the past has over how you think, act, and respond to the world. It influences our life choices, so that that we get drawn to people and projects that are patently out of alignment with our highest good.

Sadly, that is why we do everything we can to hold on to them–like getting involved in destructive relationships. Even with all our griping, we are not likely to leave without a lot of outside help (friends, counseling,

1

even the courts), and serious inner change. Our conditioning has shackled our mind and body and created a seemingly unalterable present and future by shutting us off from our own higher wisdom and divine love.

It's hard to have faith that your future will be different—and yet it can be. You are not here to suffer (as many of us have been told), but rather to work on ourselves, to break free of old, destructive belief systems, and embrace love and joy. For your own growth, you need to free up this energy. Given a chance, you can do to transform your past.

Healing the past most effectively requires releasing the *root cause* of your unwanted or outworn behavior by changing the event itself; but how can you change what has already happened? After all, the past is the past. It is impossible to go back and reshape it without using a time machine. That is true—in one sense. If your father beat you when you were a child, you can't change that reality. But—and this is a big BUT—you can change its impact *inside of you.*

Think of this process as looking at a photo album of past events. A trauma is a not a photo of a past event, but an actual experience still alive in your inner world. It's not "past", but "present". When you clear that trauma though, it becomes a memory, a mere photo of an experience. Now it is truly "past".

In order for change to occur, you need a safe environment—surroundings that encourage you to grow at your own speed, as you feel comfortable, without criticism, judgment, or pressure. This is extremely important. Being browbeaten to make changes may force some level of transformation, but not when it is accomplished in fear and unhappiness. You've had enough of that. Instead, I invite you to experience change in love and joy.

The process of healing starts with childhood issues because, not only is it the easiest time period to access, it usually has the greatest "juice". Your physical survival as a child depended on fitting in with your family structure, by cultivating behaviors that were acceptable in your environment, and eliminating the ones that might leave you unloved, hurt, or abandoned, either emotionally or physically. That may have meant submitting to awful physical, sexual or emotional abuse because there was simply no other way of being nurtured or staying alive.

In doing so, you unintentionally disconnected yourself from your Higher Self, and closed down critical parts of yourself (whether it was your heart, your spirit, or your intuition) and you focused most your life force on getting your survival needs met.

Being yourself was not acceptable.

Now that you have grown up, the pain from those childhood traumas and needs still remains embedded in your emotional body, quiescent until some event triggers it, like marrying an alcoholic, or an abusive, or neglectful spouse. When those childhood triggers get activated, the same fears you experienced as a child rushes back, as potent now as they were then—and you react in the same way. Gone are any adult behaviors and resources; you become lost in the past. You may even regress and act like a child, especially when the memory is severe, such as suddenly recovered sexual abuse memories.

To demonstrate: One of the most stressful situations you can face is visiting your family, particularly at the holidays. It is a rare person who can remain an adult (no matter how old you are) under the onslaught of parental attitudes and criticisms, and your childhood conditioning or fears. You easily drop right back into your childhood behavior, no matter what you would prefer. Afterward, you feel angry, frustrated, and disgusted with yourself for having gotten trapped again—even though you're an adult!

Blame your survival instinct.

The oldest part of your brain, the medulla, governs the flight/fight instinct. It is always operating for your Inner Child (ages two to eleven), who *never* feels totally safe, and is always on alert. Every event, large or small, is judged according to that *Child's* need to survive. When you find yourself in what the Child perceives as a dangerous emotional or physical situation, its survival behavior kicks in, and you lose any adult perspective.

Your Child does not possess the psychological makeup to make adult choices. That would be too dangerous. Only you, a fully functioning adult, can do that. It's only when you break free of your Child's fight/flight survival instinct, that you can make decisions based on adult values and understanding, rather than childhood fears and needs.

It's time to create appropriate adult behaviors by releasing those constrictive beliefs, emotional needs, and fears. We'll start by creating alternatives to those early behaviors.

Every experience in your life creates neuron pathways inside your brain and nervous system. The more intense the emotion surrounding an event, the more hormones flood through your body, and the stronger the pathway that is created or reinforced. It's like learning a new skill; the first few times you're slow and uncoordinated, as the brain's neurons form a new pathway; but with each repetition of the skill, the path is strengthened, and you become faster and more adept. (Think of learning to drive or ride a bike.)

So it is with memory. Every time you recall an emotional event, with all of the concomitant emotions flooding your body, you strengthen that pathway. Altering that memory through the process of meaningful, focused self-transformation closes off that path and creates another one.

When you clear a traumatic memory, you release trapped energy at every level of your being. It's like clearing out an abscess. First you feel a sharp pain, as the emotion (for instance, anger or sadness) pours out of you; then you feel a wonderful sense of relief as the abscess is finally cleansed of its toxins (the memory transformed).

The reconstructed memory, instead of triggering the familiar emotional states (fear abandonment, loss, rage, shame, etc.), flows into new pathways of love, forgiveness, relaxation, and peace, allowing healing to begin. This simple process removes, bit by bit, the terror and power of the past from your life. Each time that happens, profound changes ripple throughout all levels of your being—from your heart and mind to your physical body and even your soul. As your body readjusts and realigns to accommodate the new feelings, you take another step toward transformation.

With each memory that you clear, space opens inside you for something else to flow into you, things you may not believe you deserve—healing, joy and love.

When you are feeling traumatized or scared, your energy contracts into a protective stance. It's very difficult to be open to change. On the other hand, healing transformation is expansive, allowing you to shed old fears, traumas, behaviors, and patterns more easily and replace them with gentle, deep healing. The key to the whole process of self-transformation is *love*. Love does not brook hate or self-denigration. It accepts; it makes no judgment. It just is.

That leads to forgiveness—of yourself, first, and, later on, of others. By forgiving yourself for your flaws, you begin to create a space for love to enter you. The more you forgive yourself for your attitudes, feelings, actions, and judgments, the more you can feel self-acceptance. With that acceptance comes tolerance and love, and with love, inner resistance and self-dislike drain away. Your triumphs over your past conditioning can be measured in the gains you perceive in your self-wisdom, self-love, and the practice and manifestation of your higher purpose.

Let's talk about *perfection*. We all have our own concept of what perfection is, based on our family backgrounds, but we all agree on one thing: we personally aren't perfect. Actually, I'd like to let you on a little secret: None of us is perfect, no matter how much our parents and other people try to convince you and me that they are (but not you). Unless they're Jesus or Buddha (or the Dalai Lama), perfected beings just don't exist on this planet.

Since we're not perfect, and the chances of becoming so are as remote as virgin birth, where does that leave us? Maybe it's important to rethink the word "perfect." Some people say that everything, including us, is perfect at every moment. Their point is that it's useless to strive to reach an amorphous, unrealistic ideal, which can only make us feel worse, and focus on where we are right now.

For me, "perfection" is the movement toward expressing your Life Purpose; therefore, whatever you do that moves you in that direction is *perfection*. And the place to start is by forgiving yourself for not being perfect. Every time you forgive yourself for that, you do more to break your conditioning than all the recriminations you can heap upon yourself. (Remember, change comes with acceptance, not fear.) The first few times may be difficult, but with practice, you'll be amazed at how easy it becomes to forgive your flaws, and in doing so, embrace change.

Sometimes you may wish you could return to your previous life because it was easy and safe, no matter how dysfunctional it was. However, once you step onto the path to self-healing, it is almost impossible to regress. You can try to halt your progress by making yourself sick, or having accidents, but that can't halt your growth. It will proceed anyway because your soul wants desperately to break out of its emotional and mental prison and manifest its Life Purpose.

You may wonder whether you dare continue your self-transformation because the consequences really are earthshaking. In fact, you will become an entirely different person, much closer to the person envisioned by your Higher Self. If, after working through the exercises in this book, you have reached some modicum of self-acceptance, you will have created an enormous potential for your own evolution toward your Life Purpose.

Let's now look beyond the traumas of childhood. Many of our behaviors, patterns, and fears don't arise from this lifetime. That means in your spiritual journey you must go back to those lives that impact your life now, whether in your choice of family, childhood abuse, or the blocks that cut you off from the knowledge and love you need for your continued growth. Usually, these lifetimes have complementary or similar stories to your present lifetime–if you abused someone in a past life, she or he did the some to you in the next one, and so forth; or you may be continuing the same behavior lifetime after lifetime. You're trapped in a rut.

By going back and rectifying those events, you begin untangling the psychic snarl of abuse between yourself and others. Moreover, as you do that deep soul level healing, it creates a vortex of healing for all the other people involved in that lifetime or event, although you may not ever know what kind of healing they receive.

Finally, you must remember that change does not happen overnight. In traditional psychotherapy, talking about an issue helps the client incrementally dismantle it, like pulling one pebble at a time out of a wall. In inner work, the pebbles come in handfuls, so the edifice of resistance and old patterning can collapse sooner, though always under the guidance and wisdom of your Higher Self. Change also takes persistence–in the face of the unpleasant, sad, shameful, and angry feelings that arise within you and in others.

The techniques that I describe in this book are profoundly useful strategies for change. They all involve releasing trapped energy and transforming yourself by using healing vibrations and love.

Through this self-healing process you can reclaim your lost inner power, wisdom, and self-esteem, and manifest your Life Purpose.

CHAPTER 2
THE FIVE SELVES

Many traditions postulate that everything on earth can be broken down into four basic elements. Those four elements do not describe the scientific structure of objects, but rather their intrinsic nature, which correlates closely with the essence of your four mortal selves.

Earth is physical, tangible, and solid–which describes your *physical body*. Air is intangible, light, and invisible–which is *the aura,* that invisible energy shield around each of us. Water is fluid, changeable, and deep– which can be identified with your *emotions*. Fire is hot, burning and incisive–which aptly describes your *mind*. Finally, the fifth body is the quintessence of all these other bodies combined–the Soul or *Higher Self.*

Before you took a body, your soul chose the conditions of your life-to-be, the family it intended to join, the kind of childhood and other life experiences it wanted you to have, the karma it chose to pay back and the life lessons you needed to learn. It also gathered the resources required to manifest your Life Purpose. After all that, the soul decided what qualities you could use to provide those life lessons, karmic paybacks, and spiritual growth (it's a little like choosing one item from Column A, two from Column B, etc.).

When the five parts work together, as they did for the first few moments when you first arrived on this earth at birth, you have congruence. Everything is in alignment; and there is an easy flow back and forth between the soul and those other parts of you. You feel connected to the divine, continuously bathed in tremendous love and joy, and easily able to manifest your work.

The strains of the life situation, however, pull you out of your inner alignment. Then you become wracked with doubts, anger, frustration, shame, so that you get caught in the conflicting needs of the four mortal selves. It's like being behind a four-horse chariot team that is out of control–horses pull every which way. This leads to inner conflict and turbulence, especially if one part tries to dominate the others. Think of the mind, which denigrates or cuts off the physical body and emotions; or the emotional body, which uses manipulation to remain in control.

When that split occurs, there can be no harmonious blending of energies and purpose. Instead, there is internal dissension, frustration and stress. Some of your stresses arise in childhood; others have been embedded in the soul for lifetimes. The result is a clash and cacophony between the four elements. This internal warfare does an excellent job of keeping you fractured and unfocused, so that you cannot hear anything clearly. You forget your connection to your soul, which could and would bring you into balance–if you could even remember that it exists. You need to be restored to balance.

The surest mechanism for healing is love. Not the love most of us know–a love contaminated by needs, fears, and beliefs (your own and others)–but a transcendent, godly, expansive love that fills us with joy and delight, and makes us glad to be ourselves. This love can only shine clearly through us when we are in complete balance. This is the gold vibration–the harmonious blending of the elements inside us (see Chapter 5).

Most of us operate far below this gold level. Our internal emotional and mental blocks pull down our energy and keep us off balance. The longer they remain, the more destructive they become, not only to our energy, but to our physical body, where they manifest as disease, like cancer cells invading healthy tissue.

Since all of the bodies inhabit the same space together, and are designed to work as one unit, releasing old patterns in one body causes an energetic shift in all of them–and leads to the rebuilding of a communication that was disrupted over the years.

Let us examine each of the five bodies in detail.

The Etheric Body

The etheric body or aura, is a flexible invisible energy sheath (like air), that extends out about a foot and a half from the body. It acts as a buffer for the physical body against the world. This force field expands and contracts, according to your mood and situation. Your aura is the most acute of your body parts because, consisting of very light vibrational energy, it can detect the truth behind a person's obfuscating words and confusing emotions.

Have you ever met someone and taken an instant dislike to them—a feeling later proven accurate? That is because both your aura and theirs touched, and your aura d1dn't like what it sensed from the other person.

Your aura tries to communicate what it has sensed through its language of comfort/discomfort. Whenever you feel some kind of emotional reaction to someone, such as uneasiness or delight, your aura has "spoken" to you. Unfortunately, many of us rarely pay attention to our aura's very accurate comments.

The more you tune in to your aura's messages (sensations), the more you can start to trust the information that you receive. Most of us lost this faculty as children. You denied what you could see was true, and accepted what you were told by others, suppressing your own wisdom for the sake of family unity and/or personal survival.

A good example is growing up in an alcoholic family. Many children of alcoholics report seeing their father drunk or passed out, and yet being told by their mother that daddy wasn't drunk, just sleeping or overtired. So what do they believe—their eyes or the authority figure? This is the kind of situation that makes children crazy. They *must* reject the truth and accept the word of the authority figure for the sake of surviving in the household. As a result of growing up in families like that, you don't dare rely on your innate wisdom.

Being your first line of connection with other people, your aura collects a lot of alien energies (i.e., not yours), that end up clogging your energy field. Since it is invisible, you are rarely aware of the debris it picks up. Here's what I mean: Suppose you're sitting next to a hungry person who's obsessed with buying a hamburger. As your aura brushes up against his, you absorb some of his desire, and though you're neither hungry nor interested in meat, suddenly you develop an insatiable craving for a hamburger. That person's aura has unwittingly contaminated you. Your aura holds on to many emotions like these without knowing it, so that after a long time, it's hard to find space for yourself. Just as your physical body needs cleansing when you get dirty, your aura needs to be cleaned out, as well.

Anyone who comes into your personal space touches your aura. There are some people you actually may want to invite into your space (like lovers, family members, friends). Often, other people intrude in your space (all of the above, plus outsider like coworkers, bosses, strangers on the street) without your permission, especially if you have let them in before (usually by habit or belief that you must do so).

Their energy residue can linger with you for years, even lifetimes. Sometimes, that energy is neutral or loving; more often it's critical, judgmental, shaming, guilt-making, and/or hateful. When you clean out your aura (see Chapter 4), you can remove that unwanted alien energy. Otherwise, it remains inside you for years, affecting or blocking you in some way.

Here's an example: when someone threatens you with a raised fist, he also takes his energy and slams it into your aura, usually at your solar plexus, your power center. When you feel the blow, you flinch, even though he *never physically* hit you. His energy now remains in your aura as a energy bruise until you remove it.

I met a woman who complained that she couldn't conceive of the idea of having "space" for herself. Her whole life had been devoted to taking care of others, whether with money, or time, or responsibility; she had never been without other people's energies in her space. Cleaning out her aura, she reported, was one of the most eerie experiences she had ever had; she had never felt "alone" in her own space. After getting over the strangeness of being the only person in her space, she was thrilled.

The Physical Body

Your physical body (the tangible envelope of the mind, emotions, and soul) is made of very dense energy called earth. It exists in time and space, and it must follow the physical laws of the planet (no teleportation, so far). When you die, your body returns back to the earth to be recycled (or would if we didn't embalm our bodies and lock them into incorruptible plastic caskets).

The aura creates the physical body according to the soul's instructions. Imagine the aura as a kind of fairly flexible armor or template. Inside it, the body is created, cell by cell, conforming to that template, like jewelry being cast from a mold. For example, if your physical body is handicapped, that is because your soul created the body's template that way.

Just like your aura, your physical body collects and stores an enormous amount of energy, usually negative, first from negative images thrown at it—by yourself as well as others ("Why are you so fat? Why couldn't you have been taller? Or your breasts bigger?" etc.), and then from sexual, emotional or physical abuse. Once the physical body's bruises healed, you may assume that the trauma has vanished, but in fact, it remains embedded in whatever organs were traumatized.

After enough traumas accumulate in your physical body, they become so intense that your body must start releasing them in some way; that is called illness or disease. Instead of recognizing the illness for what it is—a cry for help to get rid of the painful energies—you look at the body as an enemy that threatens your existence. Eventually, these negative energies can become too much for the body to bear and manifest as a life-threatening disease. The most common such process is cancer. (Some cancers have a genetic component, but mostly the genetic predisposition is just that—a predisposition, not a guarantee. If you live a life in which you clear your physical and emotional blocks continually, you will be less likely to trigger those genetic cancer markers. It's *all* your choice.

> *Sephronia[1] gained extra weight as a result of menopause. She attempted to lose those pounds for fifteen years with every kind of diet, pill, and exercise plan, while continuing to denigrate and excoriate her body for being so heavy. As a result of those negative attacks, her body has suffered one illness after another, which causes her to hate it even more, and eventually, she developed cancer and had to have radiation and chemotherapy. This was not a happy body.*

To release those negative energies from those invisible but potent wounds requires a complete attitude shift and an acceptance of the body as it is—in other words, flooding it with self-esteem and love.

It doesn't help that certain religions conceive of the physical body as evil, no good, worthless, and something to transcend. For millennia, it was considered good form to chastise the flesh with hair shirts, fasting, flagellation, or other tortures.

That attitude persists today, if not those harrowing methods. Many of you wish you could occupy your mind, your aura, your spirit—everywhere but your body. Not surprisingly, you may tend to spend a lot of time out of your body, letting it run on automatic pilot. What does *that* mean?

Here's a common example: If you take a long drive, when you get to your destination, you may remember almost nothing you saw along the route. You zoned out—you left your body and went somewhere else. By vacating the body, you are not aware of what's going on in or around you. When you bump into objects, that's because you're not there to guide your body. That's when you can get hurt or make unwise decisions that lead you into physical or emotional danger.

---

1. All examples are composites of clients, and names have been changed.

With that kind of background, it's no surprise that of all the selves, your physical body requires the most healing work and needs the most love. By acknowledging that your Higher Self chose this physical body for you, perhaps you can begin to make an effort to come into harmony with it.

The Emotional Self

Emotion's element is water, with its movement and changeability, that can release and transmute all the frozen energies, and rinse away the blocks, fears, and old painful emotions, so there is room left for love, the vibration of self-transformation, to enter.

Not suprisingly, the emotional body's most powerful emotional is love–love of self and love of others. It is not logical, literal, or organized, but expresses depth, caring, and empathy. As love fills you, you open up like a flower, while feelings like fear, sadness, and anger close you down.

A baby is a bundle of love. Yet as it grows, it needs to have love reflected back to it, usually from its mother, to retain that sense of love. If the baby doesn't get enough love, or love is intermittent or missing, the impact on the child's well-being is tremendous. It is forced to turn its focus outside of itself, seeking people and situations that can provide it with love—in any way possible.

Not surprisingly, the symbol for the emotional self is the Inner Child, who lives in your heart. She or he governs your actions and behavior, usually unconsciously. Their emotional needs and fears govern how you will interact with others–whether you will face them with openness and optimism, fear and despair, hatred and aggression and/or manipulation and game-playing.

Logic can neither sway nor bludgeon the Child into submission because its emotional needs far outweigh your mind's arguments. If you got off the phone after a painful conversation with your lover and you feel miserable (i.e., abandoned, unloved), eating chocolate numbs the pain a little. (Chocolate is a natural antidepressant.) The Child's emotional cry for nurturance (via food) overrides your logic at the moment, but the mind gets its revenge with its continual negative mental barrage.

Whenever your Inner Child is out of control, the most potent antidote is to fill it with intense, overwhelming love. When that happens, you start to clear away the painful patterns that keep you locked in non-loving beliefs and behaviors. In this way, you not only begin to disconnect the Inner Child from his or her fears, but you open yourself up for your own nurturance.

The Mental Self

The symbol of the mind is fire. The quality of fire is brilliant, biting, and incisive. The tarot symbolizes the mind as a sword. Consider the purpose of a sword. It's sharp, and it can shred or slice someone to ribbons.

Remember the childhood chant: "Sticks and stones will break my bones, but names will never hurt me"? Not true! Words are far more destructive than sticks and stones. Physical bruises heal, but the effects of ridicule and cutting words remain, destroying a person's self-esteem now and in the future.

You think, analyze, and express yourself through your mental body. It keeps you from turning into emotional mush. The mind understands concepts, ideas, and perceptions. It extrapolates and interpolates; it's logical, it has opinions and attitudes. You can call it your ego or personality. It is also prone to rigid thinking, narrow-mindedness, "illogical logic," holding an opinion long after evidence proves that it's specious and destructive. When people say, "stop being so emotional," they're saying, "get back into your mental body." The mind has cachet. It is okay to hang out there, to be "rational" like Mr. Spock. Lots of logic, lots of (mis)perception–but no heart.

In its arrogance, your mind thinks it is in charge, even though it is really controlled by the childhood fears and needs of the emotional body. It formulates its world view according to how well you got your emotional needs met from the people and events of our early life. That means your belief system may be badly skewed, but you can't tell unless you examine it clearly and dispassionately. For that, you may need an outside source (like a counselor). An example of such rigid narrowness is a fundamentalist (of any religion).

What kinds of beliefs have you incorporated into your mind? Here are just two of the many you may hold (both very common):
- The world is a dangerous place.
- You don't deserve love and you'll never be worthy it of it.

Both of those beliefs are self-propagating: you'll do everything to prove them to yourself in your life.

Nor does your mind believe in or accept the love the Higher Self would like to give you.

What if you could change one of your beliefs? You can. It takes time and energy to reprogram yourself–and the willingness to do it.

If your mind is made up, it takes a lot of words to chip away at the belief in order to alter it. That's the basis of counseling. As beliefs fall away, the more flexible you become, and the more able to make adjustments in your belief system. When you realize you're wrong about an idea, and your mind absorbs that lesson and adjusts its thinking, you loosen more barriers restricting your mind–whether they are self-imposed or not. (Obvious examples are racism and gay marriage–our attitudes have markedly shifted about both in over the past 50 years.)

The Spiritual Body

Your immortal spiritual body (soul) is the creator of your existence on earth. I call it the **Higher Self** . Since this wise part of you resides *outside* the physical body (six to eight inches above your head), it has a much higher and clearer perspective of your life, free of the rigid thinking of the mental self, beyond the passion and fears of the emotional self, and the pain of the physical body. Intuitions are messages from the Higher Self, or even from the divine (god/goddess).

The spiritual self is the lodestone around which the other parts of you revolve; this part of you knows exactly the words or images that will guide you toward your spiritual path. To fulfil your Life Purpose, you need to align very closely with your spiritual self. It has your well-being in mind at all times, and will *never* try to hurt you.

LOVE

When your body is out of balance, you cannot feel love, or you may feel it in a distorted way because it cannot come into you freely. As you heal your past and release blocks, you open a space for that love to pour into you, undiluted and unadulterated.

Even though the four mortal selves may have a difficult time experiencing love because of all the distractions or blocks in their way, your Higher Self loves you unconditionally, if you will only allow yourself to accept and feel that love.

When the four elements (earth, air, fire, and water) combine together in a balanced way, they achieve a special quality called "gold." Think of yourself in the same way. When you bring the four bodies into balance, they radiate a gold vibration throughout you and everyone else around you, that feels wonderful, loving, and godly.

CHAPTER 3
RESOURCES FOR THE JOURNEY

In any journey, particularly a spiritual one, there must be a beginning. Ours begins with the Oversoul, that part of us that separated in innocence from the Godhead/Source[2] aeons ago. The Oversoul coordinates all of its subordinate lifetimes, those myriads of lives in every culture, and country, as part of its quest to experience every aspect of the human condition and gain the wisdom necessary return to Source.

In each of our many lives, as we struggled toward self-understanding and wisdom, we made decisions and performed deeds which created karma (cosmic balance sheet) that needed to be dealt with, in that lifetime or in later lifetimes.

It would be nice to say that the soul learns and moves on, but usually, it remains stuck on the same issue, struggling with it lifetime after lifetime like a needle stuck in a record groove, until you can finally resolve them. By discovering the cause of your reactions, and facing your own unconscious or unresolved flaws such as greed, impatience, jealousy, fear, or anger, or by dissolving the past life hooks that still twist inside you, you can step closer to achieving balance and healing.

For example, instead of reacting in a hostile manner to someone who irritates you, you might realize that he or she is acting as your mirror, providing you with an opportunity to look at the cause of your reaction and get rid of it.

Karmic issues, on the other hand are not simple lesson, but major obligations that require serious spiritual resolution, usually paying the debt in some way (see Chapter 14). For that you really need help and support. You can't do it alone. Luckily assistance is available from many high-level resources more than eager to help you on your journey.

---

2. Godhead (I use this term because it is neutral–I do not advocate for a male or female supreme being, just the "God"/Source energy.

In all the work that is described in this book, I will be calling on the assistance of many kinds of beings. If you have trouble with any of these concepts, consider them and the processes as metaphorical. You will achieve the same results.

HIGHER SELF

The first of these resources is your own Higher Self, whose help is integral to any self-transformation. The Higher Self is your wise, immortal soul, that oversees your life. It sees you clearly (warts and all), knows everything about you, and yet wants nothing more than your greater well-being. It acts as the intermediary between the Divine and you.

Your Higher Self is your most important partner in your inner work. Not being influenced by outsiders or your mind, or overwhelmed by your fears and needs, it can guide you through the arcane and convoluted territory known as the unconscious, to the exact memory with which you need to work, and bring you safely home through the process.

Since the Higher Self lives above your head, it is far enough away from the physical body to hear divine wisdom clearly, and pass it on to you–or it would if you could hear its messages without interference or judgment, particularly from your mind, which constantly judges, analyzes, argues, comments, and just never shuts up! Some kind of meditational practice that stills your mind's chatter allows you to hear your Higher Self's quiet, clear voice.

There may be times when you acquire a significant insight about something that seems impossible to know, given the information available. In those instances, the Higher Self has managed to slide an intuition past your ever-vigilant (but barriered) mind to give you the information you need to make a wise, though not necessarily informed, decision (*informed* and *wise* are **not** the same).

Besides your chattering mind, someone else's energy can obstruct that connection between your Higher Self and you. The most common culprits are your parents, who created that blockage originally to control your thoughts and behaviors when you were a child. Though they did it unconsciously, its unwitting effect was to turn you away from your Higher Self and your own wisdom–and listen only to them.[3]

More karmically dangerous are spiritual intruders–the religious leaders and teachers who impose control over their flock, such as the

---

3   Children are very open and usually blurt out whatever they feel. They learn very quickly that such "truth-telling" is NOT acceptable.

fundamentalists, creators of cults or sects, and other religious fanatics. They don't encourage independent thinking or access to higher wisdom, nor do they have your best interests at heart. Their purpose is control, and a most effective method is to cut you off from your Higher Self, so you get only their information. Their victims/followers are truly "brainwashed." Until you clean these people out of your space, you will not be able to access your Higher Self.

Evolved teachers encourage you to think for yourself and tend to use humor or irreverence to jolt you out of your mental blindness. Such a teacher helps you find your own wisdom and brings you in touch with your Higher Self.

When others block us from our Higher Self, they can convince us that we are unworthy of love and compassion, except as they decree, so that we tend to imagine ourselves as incomparably worse than we actually are. That belief was programmed into us as children, when we tried to get our own needs fulfilled. This belief is *completely false*. Our Higher Self always loves us. No matter what kinds of arguments our mind concocts to discourage us ("No one will love me if they find out about the 'real me',"), they are all untrue. They only make us feel even more in need of outside guidance and care (gladly provided by these religious leaders).

Many of us then feel ashamed to face our Higher Self, believing that we will be judged harshly for our failings. Quite the opposite! You need to remember your Higher Self *really does* know you, inside and out. If only you will give it a chance, your Higher Self would like to shower you with love.

Love is always available to you, whether you realize it or not. By connecting with your Higher Self, you create a bridge over which you can begin to accept your birthright of unconditional and unstinting love. Once you can feel the love your Higher Self dearly wants to give you, it becomes easier for you to accept it from others, both human and divine. Moreover, you begin to feel safe enough to start reclaiming lost or hidden parts of yourself–such as your self-esteem and your sense of empowerment.

You may have difficulty facing your traumas, for fear that what gets dredged up might be too overwhelming (that's your Inner Child's fear). Your Higher Self has no such qualms. It knows how much you really can handle (and you'll be amazed at how much that is). Besides, it knows what the payoff will be–wisdom, healing, acceptance, and love.

How does the Higher Self help you?

- It is dispassionate, compassionate, loving and wise, seeing you without judgment.
- Being detached from your personality, it can give you perspective on what's happening, if you allow yourself to hear it.
- It serves as the loving mediator between divine wisdom and you.
- Knowing everything that has happened to you, it can guide you into those deep places of pain and anguish.
- It always has your best interests at heart. No other person has that, including your parents.
- It can help you recognize and release karmic issues, and complete unfinished business.
- In every instance where the Higher Self participates in the healing process, it gives support, stability, and strength to your work.

Jenny was a compulsive overeater. In one therapy session, she asked her Higher Self to take her to the cause of her overeating. A memory suddenly flashed into her mind of her mother screaming at her for not finishing her meal; her mother said she worked herself to the bone to provide food for her children, who were ungrateful and uncaring. Jenny began to eat compulsively from then on, for she had figured out that her mother would love her only if she cleaned her plate. For Jenny, not eating her food equaled withheld love).

With her Higher Self's help, Jenny began to reprogram her memory, by asking for forgiveness from her body and mind for not finishing her food. As a result, her compulsive overeating disappeared. In a later discussion with her mother, Jenny learned that her mother, who grew up poor and hungry in the Depression, equated lack of food with lack of love (by her parents), and vowed always to provide enough food (i.e., love) for her children. (Isn't it amazing how motives get misinterpreted down through the generations?)

The Higher Self is also essential for any past life work. You might feel a little uncomfortable or embarrassed about what you find in a past life journey, or whether you will even sense anything. Just relax. Your Higher

Self will do its job of guiding you to the pertinent event, and also explain the lessons learned (or not) from the past lifetime, as well as any karmic debts due.

Without your Higher Self, your work will be much harder and sometimes scarier; with it, you may begin to realize that you're not all alone in the world.

Besides the Higher Self, there are other resources can call on for help.

GUARDIAN ANGEL

Most religious or spiritual traditions teach the concept of Guardian Angels or spirit guardians. Even if you do not come from such a tradition, believing in an angelic guardian of some type that can support you is very comforting.

Your Guardian Angel is a being who has chosen to attach itself to you as your invisible companion. We each have one, or even several Guardian Angels, depending on our needs and desires. Like your Higher Self, it has your best interests at heart, but unlike your Higher Self, it is not part of you. Sometimes, they are people who loved us while they were alive, like grandparents, who watch over us again in discarnate form. Others are souls who earn extra karmic points for helping us in our life work before they reincarnate. You can also ask to get a Guardian Angel at any time.

Like your Higher Self, your Guardian Angel also provides support, but its major purpose is to protect and help you in your work. Having a Guardian Angel is almost as valuable as having your Higher Self–but not quite.

Though your Higher Self always speaks your own wisdom, your Guardian Angel only has its wisdom to give you, not yours–and your own wisdom is always best.

Children are very much aware of Guardian Angels; they call them their invisible friends, who help them maneuver through their young lives and provide loving companionship.

ANGELS

Finally you can call on angels. Angels are light beings of a much higher order who are part of the Divine and do its will. There are an infinite number of angels who, at your summons, will gladly lend a hand in your life. They do not remain with you for any extended period of time unless it is necessary, but come when needed. When you need some extra high-level assistance, angels bring both divine power and divine blessing into your Process. You always can call on an angel for help in releasing your problem.

We can call on the Archangels as well as the regular angelic legions. This is very important when something comes up that terrifies you. Archangel Michael wields a sharp sword that can quite effectively chop out toxic energies or drive away evil or unwanted people. Having someone of the stature of Archangel Michael to protect or defend you from childhood abusers is enormously reassuring.

Not being part of you like the Higher Self, angelic forces speak with divine authority. That means they can heal or mitigate your karmic issue instantly, if they feel you have atoned enough, or let you finish working it out in this lifetime.

> *Leon discovered that he had endured particularly bad childhood physical abuse because he had run a boys school in a previous lifetime where he starved and brutalized his charges. He chose this life to atone for that behavior. He asked his Higher Self for help in dissolving any more karma, but his Higher Self recommended that Leon call in an angel. The angel deemed that he had suffered enough for his previous abuse and released the residual atonement.*

The following exercise will help you connect with your Higher Self. You can substitute the Guardian Angel for your Higher Self. The steps are the same.

During this exercise, I am sure your mind will be chattering away–arguing, negating. One of its most common tactics is to deny that you're sensing or seeing or feeling anything–that any sensations you do experience are all in your mind. And, by the way, this whole exercise is nonsense, and nothing's going to work, etc., etc. Does this sound familiar? Whenever you hear that mental negation, simply say, "Thank you." That tends to shut your mind up, at least for a moment.

There is no right or wrong form for your Higher Self, just whatever you perceive. In fact, from one session to another, the Higher Self may change shape and dimension. If you don't see or sense your Higher Self this time, you might later on, as you become more trusting and open.

EXERCISE

Meeting your Higher Self or Guardian Angel

1. Sit in a chair, eyes closed. Get comfortable. Put on soft music. Breathe slowly and deeply four to five times to put yourself into alignment with this exercise.

2. Imagine that your Higher Self is coming up to you and stand behind or beside you. Let your Higher Self put his/her hand on your shoulder. Imagine the pressure of their hand on your body, and also the love going down your body from its hand. Notice I said "imagine". You may not sense anything, but you can *imagine* all kinds of things. Nevertheless, I can tell you that you are soon likely to actually sense a presence beside/behind you.

3. Ask your Higher Self to come around and face you. What does he/she look like? Higher Selves come in many shapes, sizes, and dimensions. Some may look like gods and goddesses; others may look just like you. Others appear simply as energy shapes, while some can only be detected as invisible but tangible presences that you sense.

4. Ask your Higher Self what it would like to say to you, and if it has a gift to give you. Your Higher Self rarely has the opportunity to speak to you directly, unimpeded by your mind. Whatever it says or gives you, no matter how odd-sounding, thank your Higher Self. If you receive a gift, ask your Higher Self how to use it. You may be surprised, once you've come back to outer reality, how insightful its message is.

5. When you're finished, open your eyes and come back, remembering that you can go back to visit your Higher Self at any time. It is always there.

Now that you have met your Higher Self, you can face your unknown and perhaps terrifying inner world with the knowledge that you aren't alone.

CHAPTER 4
PRESENT TIME

In order to transform the past, we need to be grounded in the present. It's like having a rope solidly anchored before rappelling down a cliff face.

Let's suppose you need to make a decision about an issue (changing your job, a new relationship, moving, etc.). Although your mind provides all sorts of logical arguments for or against it, the real decision is made by your emotional heart (Inner Child) and focuses only on one concern: what will keep you safe and loved?

An adult decision requires balance between mind and heart: the mind's perspicacity, perspective, and acumen, and the heart's sense of happiness, fulfillment and delight, unfettered by childhood fears, tempered with the wisdom of the Higher Self. That comes only when you get unstuck from the past, and make your decision based on the *present*.

For many of us, the present can be an enormous surprise because we've rarely spent much time here, locked into our past, ruled by all our doubts, fears and memories. Bringing yourself into the present makes it much easier for your adult to make an appropriate decision.

PRESENT TIME

Let's begin with present time. How much of you is in the present? What exactly does *that* mean?

If your childhood patterns are controlling you, if you are locked into a certain belief system, or if you live in fear of some sort, very little of your essence is in present time. Your past or your future (such as money fears/relationship worries) govern you.

Many of us remain trapped by some traumatic or upsetting event(s) that occurred in the past. Given the opportunity, you could probably put your finger on events that changed your life—rape, sexual abuse, the death of someone close, combat experience, or some kind of endangerment qualify. Everything in your life since then has been colored by that defining moment. You cannot ignore its consequences in your life. Moreover, every time you think of it, you trap energy in it.

For example, if as a child you were beaten by your father, you're holding on to a lot of energy around those experiences (they're not memories; they're still alive in you and qualify as *traumas*). And whenever you remember (i.e., relive) it, more of your energy gets trapped. It's like a grain of sand irritating an oyster's soft body. To protect itself, the oyster wraps the sand with a nacreous coating to soothe the irritation. Unable to be expelled, the grain not only remains, but its presence inside the oyster increases with every coat. That's what happens when you keep ruminating over personal trauma. Your energy accretions accumulate, but unlike the oyster, who gets a pearl at end, your energy gets trapped in a kind of black hole, and is inaccessible for other purposes.

To reclaim that energy, you need to free yourself from the control of those memories by releasing the energy trapped in them (like getting a sudden unexpected inheritance).

Before that happens, you need to bring yourself–your aura, physical body, mind, and heart–into present time. Breaking free of the bonds of the past takes work, but it's much easier if you are in *present time,* which brings any energy from past events into the present, and raises your vibrations (see Chapter 5).

Bringing those accretions into present time is like rinsing the mud off your boots after you have been splashing through a puddle. Your boots are the incident, and the mud is the accretion. Although the issue (boots) may remain (for the present), the angst (mud) built up around it goes down the drain.

> *Ardith perceived her family responsibility as a ton of clay piled on her back. The more she thought about her responsibility, the worse she felt, and the less able she was to face it, much less handle it. She felt frozen, unable to make any decisions. After a while she could barely contemplate the whole issue. When she brought it into present time, she saw (and actually felt) the heavy burden slide off her back and break into pieces on the ground.*
>
> *Bringing her image into present time released enormous trapped guilt, frustration, and anger. She still needed to work on her responsibility issue, but it was no longer encumbered by all the accretions that glued it into place. Moreover, releasing the trapped energy deflated the*

responsibility to its original size, which, overwhelming for the Inner Child, was manageable for the adult.

Once accretions are removed (common ones like parental disapproval, personal guilt, or judgments), you can focus on handling the underlying real issue. The sooner you get through the accretions, the sooner you can tackle the issue itself.

Present Time also exposes any foreign energies stuck inside you, like your parents or lovers or friends or enemies' energies. By bringing yourself into the present, anything that comes from your past can no longer remain. It can be quite a shock to discover how much of the emotional baggage you tote around belongs to other people. It's time to send all it back to its owners!

BEFORE STARTING YOUR WORK

You need to do two preliminary techniques–*Defining Your Space* and *Retrieving Your Energy*–which provide basic cleanout, and are essential for *all* the other processes. They make your work much easier.

Defining Your Space

Your aura is a flexible force field (AKA "personal space") about eighteen inches around your body.

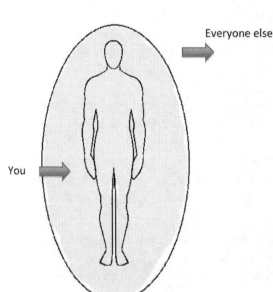

It defines your space: *I belong here, and everybody else belongs out there.* It does not isolate you from other people, since you can choose to let special friends inside–for visits. But this space belongs to only you. When you clean out your aura, you are likely to discover that you've been sharing your 3x3 home with everyone you've ever known, so there's no room for you.

Some of these people you may actually like having there (such as your lover), but they need to visit by invitation. Other people don't belong there at all. They may be drinking/user buddies from years ago, still sitting in your space, enticing you with the next hit or line or drink, long after you've gone through recovery. Their presence brings your energy down whenever you fight against the urge to use or drink. Or you might find your space crammed with the judgmental people who have criticized you all your life. There may also be people who've made you feel uncomfortable, and who hang onto you.

It's time to put an end to this party. Dig out the guests who have fallen asleep on your bed, roust the folks chatting in the living room, and the moochers rummaging through your refrigerator. Hand them their coats, shoo them out the door, and send them away—out of your space.

Many people feel very strange after doing these exercises; they suddenly feel alone after years of being unwitting hosts to a multitude of people.

The most important reason for defining your space, however, is self-love. You cannot love others until you feel safe enough to love yourself; that happens only in your space—with you and only you.

Finally, if you aren't in your body, doing your work becomes more difficult—not impossible, but harder than necessary because you won't be able access your inner resources easily, or your Higher Self—and you won't notice any changes in you.

EXERCISE

Cleaning Your Space

Before you can do any work clearing people from your space, you have to define it—which means setting up boundaries between yourself and the world. That is not only a protection for you, but also a reassurance that you have a presence.

1. Focus your attention on your aura—your invisible energy shield. Ask that it contract to eighteen inches around you and cover you from feet to head.
2. Move your hands over the aura, as if you are smoothing it over your head to underneath your feet. Be aware of what it's like being in your very own space.
3. Now it's time to clean any alien energies from your space. Imagine holding a large golden comb with 18-inch teeth. It is wider than your body, so you can hold both ends with your

hands. Use it to comb out your aura, like you're combing your hair, but do it from head to toe. Physically run your hands up and down your body in a combing motion, holding the energy comb in your hand. Do the front, then the back, and then the sides.

4. Let the combed-out energies fall onto the earth, where they can be absorbed. You may feel some strange sensations in your body as you do this exercise, or soon afterward. After all, just having your own energy in your space is quite unusual.

5. Imagine a ray of sunlight pouring through your head and into your body, filling you up to the edges of your aura. This gold energy defines the limits of your space and raises your vibration so that no one with a lower vibration can invade you easily (see Chapter 5), or push you out of your space–at least for the moment–without your permission.

Retrieving Your Energy – Energy Whistle

Since alien energy gets stuck in your aura from both recent and long-past interactions, it's only reasonable to assume that some of your energy has been left in other places, as well–and indeed it has, in every place you have lived, in your childhood, with family members, at your jobs, with friend and enemies–and all of it is locked in the past. This next technique reclaims your essence–maybe small amounts at first, but more and more as you do the exercise.

1. Close your eyes and imagine you holding an energy whistle, like an ultra-high-pitched dog whistle. Blow it to call your own energy home (and no one else's).

2. Above your head is a bowl filled with golden liquid. This is energy soap. After a few moments, the pieces of your energy will start flowing back into this bowl, to be cleansed of anyone else's cooties. They may appear or feel like snowflakes, blobs, a river of energy or light, or any other form you might imagine.

3. Give yourself about five minutes to allow your energy to come back. Then dump the bowl over your head so the energy pours into you. As your body and aura start absorbing your returning essence, you may even begin to feel like you have more shape and presence.

4. Every time you do this, you might suddenly recall memories or people from years ago. That's where your energy was trapped.

Do both of these exercises every day for maximum benefit. As you continue doing them, energies that you lost in earliest childhood will return, until finally you are more complete than you have ever been in ages.

Using The Present Time Wand

This technique requires nothing more than your imagination. You may or may not notice any body reaction as you do the technique, but there will be shifts in your energy. If you feel any kind of jolt, that's your bodies adjusting and realigning to the newly accessible energies. I consider this exercise simply one of the most effective tools in your spiritual and psychic tool kit. I use it ALL THE TIME. Using the present time wand *daily* and *before every healing session* helps you process much more easily.

1. Ask your Higher Self to give you a present time wand. It may be any shape and form you can imagine. Pick it up and hold it. Imagine your fingers curved around it. This is your present time wand. (If you want to really hold a wand, you can buy or make one.)

2. Tap your aura seven times to clean it thoroughly. Move your hand slowly outward with each tap, until your arm is at the edge of your aura (about 18 inches).

3. Tap the top of your head, your forehead, your throat, your heart, your stomach, your navel, three inches below your navel, your pubis (these are your chakras).

4. Tap your feet and hands (which have their own chakras and help with the movement of energy through your body).

5. You have now brought all of you into present time.

6. Anything that is not in present time will drop off because it cannot remain at the present time vibration. Let that energy fall to the earth to be recycled.

CHAPTER 5
ENERGY VIBRATIONS

Until now, you have been operating at a lower vibration than you could be, since your parts are out of balance and out of tune from your life experiences. Yet that was part of your master plan–to learn from these experiences and lessons you have had in your life–and then retune yourself to a higher vibration. To do that, you need to familiarize yourself with the qualities of energy.

Energy consists of two elements–vibration and frequency.

Vibrations: Sound and Clarity

Vibration indicates the *clarity* of your energy. It gives off a tone or pitch.

A muddy tone indicates blockage in your energy, while a clearer pitch indicates more free-flowing energy with fewer blocks. The kind of blocks you have indicates the kind of energy you emanate. People can detect when you are sending out good or bad vibrations, and you can feel theirs as well.

What do vibrations have to do with your inner work?

When you raise your vibration, or frequency, you shake up all those parts of you that do not vibrate at that level. It's like sending ultrasound into a kidney stone; the sound waves break up the stone so it can pass out of your body. That's what higher vibrations do.

Your vibration is magnified by emotional intensity. The stronger the emotion you express, the more intense your vibration. A lot of people believe that the more enlightened you become, the less intensity you will have. That is incorrect. It's not the *intensity* that matters, but the *clarity*.

Somebody who's very impassioned about something feels intense; if he's expressing joy around us, we feel uplifted excited, enlivened, and energized. On the other hand, somebody who spews rage or hatred is just as passionate, but his intensity makes us feel dirty, disturbed, or uncomfortable. I can't listen to rap music for that reason. The energy coming out of those songs is so full of rage that it literally hurts my body. I don't want this kind of vibration in my space.

Such a strong hurtful feeling inside you means that your energy is trapped and cannot flow freely. It's as though you're stuck in a pressure cooker, and as you get more and more enraged, your vibration intensifies–with no outlet for release–except through an explosion. The subsequent emotion feels excruciatingly painful and unpleasant–like stabbing knives. It is also extremely damaging to your physical health over a long period of time.

Body Vibrations

Besides your overall vibration, each of your bodies has its own vibratory sound, with the physical body having the lowest frequency, and the soul, the highest. Together, when they are in tune, these different tones create a musical chord, a rich tone that combines the different frequencies together into a beautiful complex balanced harmony. Whenever you fall out of harmony, you will easily sense it instantly.

Your Higher Self always vibrates at a pure pitch, but your other bodies usually express various out-of-tune sounds because of the blocks stuck in each of them. When those have been removed, their clear energies will combine to create a balanced harmony. It's a state few of us have attained, but it can be reached occasionally. There may come a time when you achieve it all the time. As you get close to that balance you feel the difference in yourself.

Once you achieve that delicate balance where the bodies create the perfect harmonic chord, it feels wonderful–joyous, expansive, and healing. This is the level of *gold*. Gold resonates at the highest vibration of all. That means whenever you fill yourself with gold, it breaks up and flushes away anything that vibrates at a lower pitch.

Being in that perfect vibration means everything moves clearly and smoothly. Your consciousness expands. You feel lighter and more joyous. You see yourself and the world more clearly and lovingly; you feel more empathy for others; and you perceive new perspectives. (If we had more people vibrating at the gold harmony level, the world would be far different.)

Frequency Levels

When you get depressed, you have much less energy available to you. Your level drops as your energy becomes trapped or immobile. If you are chronically depressed, not only do you have low energy you are also loaded with negative feelings that pull you down and cause your energy to be trapped–which makes you feel worse, and pulls your energy down more. It's a vicious cycle.

Your work, your attitudes, and the people in your life (business and personal) both create and affect your frequency, as well as the quality of your vibrations. When you were first born, you vibrated at a very high level (you are, after all, a cosmic being inhabiting a body). Then, all through childhood, your family assaulted you with disapproval, rage, shame, manipulation, guilt, judgment, blame, or neglect (as well as love), which distorted and blocked your feelings, and clogged your aura with their energies. The stronger their emotions and the younger you were, the less ability you had to dispel them. Gradually, your energy level dropped, so that you ended up vibrating at a level that reflected your belief about your self-worth (or lack of it)–and the world around you reinforced that idea.

If you hold the belief that you are not very good, it's as though you carry a sign in front of you projecting the message, "I only deserve to have those experiences that prove I'm not very good." You then create situations that reinforce that message. If you are in an abusive relationship, it was your vibration that attracted that kind of person into your life. The lower your vibration, the worse the energies, experiences, and relationships you create for yourself–whether you believe it or not (see Chapter 9).

Take codependency. If you are codependent, you have negative self-worth, and an unfulfilled need for love that you hope will be satisfied by helping others (though it never really does). As a result of giving away your energy to others, there is very little for yourself. Your vibration is muddy.

For things to change, you must demolish the inner structure that contains that negative belief–though at times you may believe that you'll never get to the end of a particular issue, but eventually, with enough work, it gets released. Consider this metaphor: cleaning up a large wet colored stain. As you wipe off one area, the liquid overruns it, but the stain is slightly weaker than it was before. With every spongeful of liquid removed, you reduce the stain's strength, bit by bit, until it's finally gone.

Every time you raise your vibration, you wipe away some amount of the toxic energies inside you. When you break that codependent need for others' approval and allow yourself to be nurtured, you raise your energy level and your vibration. As a result, you will find you have so much energy, love, and joy that you can gladly share it with others–not from lack and need and a hope of getting something back, but from abundance.

Higher Frequency

The most important effect of raising your vibrational frequency is that the structures inside you that don't match your new vibration must change as well. It's like riding a ten-speed bike. When you shift the gears on your handlebars, you force the gears on the wheel to move as well. They can't argue with you; they shift, or the bike breaks down.

This is why, whenever you do your work, it is *impossible* to regress. That can be very scary because your Higher Self's desire for change is often coupled with an equally great fear from your four non-spiritual parts, for whom change is terrifying. It helps if you let them adjust gradually to the loss of old patterns and the reclamation of lost energies. That means doing a steady process, not wholesale demolition and reconstruction. Too-fast change makes your body very upset–literally. You get sick.

I find when I do my own work that I must stop for a while and let the changes be absorbed and assimilated throughout my bodies; then I continue.

As these changes occur, and as old negative energies vanish from your life, you begin to vibrate at a higher frequency, so that whoever falls below that vibration cannot gravitate toward you, or stay around you. It's as though you have disappeared from their radar; you become invisible to them. Instead, you can attract new relationships and accept new attitudes about yourself and others that are different from what you knew before, sometimes markedly so. That can be unnerving because these new relationships are so unfamiliar.

Sickness

Under normal circumstances, your reserve of energy may be barely half of what you were born with (because your available energy is locked away in your traumas and blocks), but when you get sick, you have even less energy available, since your body is using all of it to fight off the illness. That's why any kind of activity exhausts you immediately.

Temporary sicknesses like flu and colds serve as one of the body's most efficient mechanisms for cleaning out clogged energies and raising our vibrations. The particular variety of sickness tells you where most of your blockage is: heart = chest colds, bronchitis; communication = head colds, sore throat, coughs.

Many years ago, I used to tell friends that I got a cold when I needed to clean out my energy system. They all laughed at me and called my examples mere coincidence. After a while, when I started correlating their illnesses to their energy blocks, they admitted that I might be correct. Now it's common knowledge.

Working with higher beings also helps you raise your vibration level. When you allow your Higher Self or an angel's energy into your body, you vibrate at a much higher pitch. Sometimes you can accept this vibration, and sometimes it creates enormous chaos inside you, if your energy is low. The more you can allow yourself to absorb these higher energies, the more you will raise your own vibration.

Vibration Scale

Imagine an energy scale that goes from 0-10 (below). A zero is complete evil–your own hell on earth. A ten means you are at the level of transcendence.

0	1	2	3	4	5	6	7	8	9	10
Hell	Addiction			Typical			Best			Bliss

Ten is a divine place to sit for about a minute–and that's it! Your body cannot tolerate a vibration that is too far beyond its capability, and could self-destruct if left up there too long. Luckily, it will pull your vibration back down to a bearable level almost immediately.

Even if you can tolerate a much higher dial setting, there is another problem–few people can match that vibration. The higher your vibration, the more difficult it is for people below that frequency to interact with you. If you can only attract what is at your level and above, you'll end up with devotees, not friends. How many 10's do you know? I guarantee, none. They can't survive at that level.

Raising your vibration without clearing your blocks can hurt you physically. It may trigger a cold, as your physical body tries to raise its vibration. You must clear out your psychic pores before you move your dial higher. The present time wand will help you by releasing a lot of those energies.

The best way to raise your vibration is by doing it slowly and gradually, accustoming you and your body to the changes gradually. That's why I recommend raising the dial one notch at a time, until you find a comfortable level.

In order to keep your friends and family in your life, a range of 5-6 is the best. It's a safe level for personal healing, and it helps raise the vibrations of others around you.

The other benefit of being at that level is that anyone below that level cannot bother or harm you because your vibration is too high for them. The sole exception is paying back karma.

EXCERCISE

Body Alignment

This exercise aligns your four mortal bodies with your Higher Self, so that they all vibrate at the same pitch, if only for a few moments. Every time you do this exercise, you vibrate at that higher essence level, and all of you–body, soul, mind, and heart, blend together in the way you were supposed to be on this planet.

1. You need four seats, two objects, like pillows or stuffed animals, and a shawl. Take two objects and put them on two of the seats.
2. Sit down at a third seat, wrapping the afghan around you. Clean out your aura and put yourself in present time.
3. The shawl is your aura, which you will now take off. Say, "I'm taking off my aura and leaving it here," as you drop the shawl onto the seat. Do this slowly and mindfully. Don't "imagine" this exercise. Actually move around.
4. Now, go to the first pillow, pick it up, and sit down. Say, "I am leaving my emotional body here", and imagine it going into the pillow. Stand up and put the pillow back down.
5. Go to the next pillow, pick it up, and sit down. Say, "I am leaving my mental body here," and imagine it going into the pillow. Stand up and put the pillow back down on the seat.
6. Go to the last seat (no pillow) and sit down. This is your physical body.
7. Ask your Higher Self to align your body's energy with it. Imagine your Higher Self sliding down through the top of your head and filling your body up with its Presence. *You don't have to do anything; just sit there and let your Higher Self do its job.* Your body will be vibrating at a level you haven't experienced for many years. If you start feeling aches and pains, your body

is letting you know about the places where it's blocked. (This exercise can help show you where to focus your work, as in Chapter 7.)

8. After a few moments, stand up. Your Higher Self and physical body are in alignment. Move over to the mental body, pick up the pillow and sit down; hug the pillow. Summon the mental body back inside you so the Higher Self can put it into alignment with it.

9. Your mental body may make all sorts of comments while your Higher Self does its work. Acknowledge any comments that come up (simply say, "Thank you").

10. Move to the emotional body. Repeat the same procedure. Let the Higher Self put it into alignment.

11. Sit down in your aura. Put the shawl around your body while your Higher Self aligns your energies. You might find it extremely difficult to hold the alignment for more than a few moments. That shows how blocked you are. Or you might find it quite comfortable because you've done some work on your self.

12. Now imagine a gold ball of sunlight coming down through the top of your head and filling up your body and aura. This gold energy reprograms your cells for love and joy instead of the low vibration you have had in the past–and it helps to attune your energy.

13. Open your eyes when you are done.

Vibrational Armor

The blocks and accretions you carry around with you as an adult form a kind of psychic armor that lowers your vibrations. Imagine a ship in dry dock, encrusted with barnacles, corroded, and rusty from oxidation. Your armor is also heavy, impenetrable, rigid, and hard to walk around in. It provides you with protection, as well as constricting your movements.

Wouldn't it be nice to get rid of it and start all over again with something new- free of rigidity, corrosion, and constriction?

You do need some spiritual protection for yourself–another kind of armor that is right for you now, but it can be something with a far higher vibration. Inside your heart is a high vibration energy envelope or bodysuit that your baby self had when it came onto this planet. It still exists in the very center of your heart, and you can retrieve it, and put it on now, as an spiritual and evolving adult.

1. Tap your body with the present time wand to bring your armor into present time.
2. It's time to take your armor off, piece by piece. Drop it on the ground with a clatter—your helmet, breastplate, gauntlets, etc., from head to toe. Then step away from the psychic heap on the ground. Actually, moving from one spot to another on your floor makes this exercise more tangible.
3. Dispose of that old armor. You can break it apart with a hammer, throw it in the ocean, drop it into a vat of gold liquid, have it hauled away by cosmic garbage truck, etc. You don't need it any longer.
4. Take the energy envelope out of your heart. It's an enormously flexible and expansive body suit. It will fit whatever size you are now.
5. Climb into it. Pull it over your feet and legs, arms and hands, up your torso and shoulders, over your head and face, until it covers all of you.

This new suit will protect you with the highest cosmic vibrations, free of personal contamination.

Raising Vibrations

1. Imagine the dial that goes from 0 to 10. It may have smaller gradations if you want. Ask your higher self to show you where your dial is set.
2. Reach out and raise the dial a notch. That means if you are at a 5.5, raise it to a 6.5. If that feels uncomfortable, raise it half a notch to 6.
3. Check it occasionally to make sure that the dial setting stays at that level. When you feel more comfortable, raise it a little higher. Don't go beyond 6, at least until you have done a lot of clearing work.

Having done all this preparatory work in the first five chapters, it is time to begin the actual process of *healing your past*.

CHAPTER 6
IMAGES: THE MIND

Your belief system is like the steel girders of a building that create the structure of your self. It controls the attitudes that color your perceptions and conceptions of yourself and your world. Belief systems shape your life. Some are moral or ethical systems of right and wrong, like the Golden Rule, or tenets of a particular group such as those that define you as Christian, Muslim, or Jewish, and further, as an Orthodox vs. Reform or Conservative Jew. Other beliefs are centered on a particular country or doctrine, organization, or attitude (like "The American Way," "democracy," "evangelicalism," "feminism", etc.).

Belief systems collide when both sides refuse to give up their own beliefs or acknowledge the validity of others. A belief system demands that you accept a whole set of conditions that limit the possibilities in your life. The more rigid your belief system is, the less ability you have for flexible thinking, empathy, or understanding others. Fundamentalists, for example, live in a black-and-white world, with no shades of gray. The stronger the conviction, the more energy it takes to hold that belief in place and drive away all the others. Depending on its rigidity, it's hard to see an alternate perspective, much less comprehend it.

Beliefs

We have two kinds of beliefs–macro and micro beliefs. Macro beliefs encompass societal values–moral, governmental, religious, philosophical codes for the society, of which you are a part.

Micro beliefs are person-centered, arising from family beliefs and personal experience. Just as you chose the behaviors that would provide you with the love and safety you needed in your family, so you also absorbed your family's belief system. Having learned what values were acceptable in your home, you incorporated them into your own belief structure.

If your father beat you, you may believe physical abuse is not only an acceptable way of dealing with family issues, but even an expression of love. Or perhaps you were told by a parent or adult to allow other children to play with your toys (whether you wanted to or not); though supposed to teach you about sharing, it often creates resentment and possessiveness. It inadvertently taught you about deservability (you don't deserve possessions). Such beliefs can be very pernicious; you are apt to accept them blindly because they are the only experience you have.

Macro beliefs are pretty obvious; micro beliefs are subtle and unconscious. You don't realize that you think and act according to them until something brings them into your consciousness—like being hauled off to jail for beating your wife.

Belief systems get cemented into your inner structure, first by family practices, later by religion and school, and by television shows, which continually emphasize one viewpoint or other. The *Leave it to Beaver* family—wife at home in dress and pearls, husband working—reinforced the value system of white middle-class America of the 1950s. That particular image has been thrown onto the garbage heap, as new values (both good and bad) have replaced it.

Every single decision you make reflects your belief system. If you believe you must look and act a certain way, you will. If you believe you are at the mercy of your body and mind, you are. If you hold an image of yourself as worthless, you will create worthlessness in your life. If you believe you don't deserve success, then you won't create it. Any argument to the contrary will be dismissed and devalued with comments (voiced or unvoiced) like "if you really knew me...." Being in an abusive relationship only reinforces your worthlessness.

As an adult, you need to sift through your parents' values and discover those values that are right for you. If they have done their job well (i.e., helping you be perspicacious, open to all kinds of ideas, and willing to examine yourself and your beliefs), you can recognize what feels right, and what doesn't have value for you, and you can adjust your micro beliefs to support your personal growth.

Changing Beliefs

When you look through a screen door, you don't see a clear picture of what's outside; your view is obscured slightly by the mesh. Although your *eye* sees the screen, your *mind* usually ignores its presence. Well, your belief system as a collection of many patterned screens between you and the world. With ten different screens in ten different shades and patterns in front of your eyes, it is much more difficult to discern anything clearly through them.

Because beliefs control your perceptions, they are almost impossible to change without some serious, dedicated work, to peel off your screens, one by one. That will give you more access to different viewpoints. It doesn't help that the mind is very rigid–it doesn't like new ideas. It's amazing how bizarre some of its beliefs are–and how tenaciously it holds on to them, until you actually verbalize them. That's the best way to look at what is controlling you, and you can work on changing your limited and warped beliefs, one by one.

Let's take something as controversial as being gay. If you are conservative, and your son announces that he is gay, he has shaken your belief system. Will you make a simple, black-and-white choice, according to your religious and moral beliefs, or will your decision be grounded in compassion, even it if violates your beliefs? You can do what many parents have done: disown him because of your moral conviction that being gay is a sin. That's the simplest option–and it leaves your belief system safe and intact. However, there are other choices:

1. You struggle with your love for him because of his "immoral" lifestyle, either openly or within yourself, or
2. You say, "Although I don't condone your lifestyle, I love you anyway," or
3. You accept your son wholeheartedly, no matter what he is, because he is your son.

Just wrestling with the issue is self-expanding, for it forces you to examine the screen that automatically rejects gays (and probably other groups as well). Following your belief system maybe "right" within that belief system, but if it cuts off love, it may not necessarily be the "right thing" to do.

Jesus taught that love is the most important quality of all ("Do unto others as you would have them do unto you" is a teaching many religious types have forgotten.). If you condemn someone because of his beliefs, you are committing the same sin as if someone condemned you for your beliefs. On the other hand, when you say, "This is what I believe, *but…,*" you begin to let go of a screen and release some of the energy trapped in your belief system.

It takes a lot of energy to maintain a belief. When you let it go, it creates a great shift inside. The dismantling of any internal structure immediately shifts your vibration and self-perspective, and all that energy that was locked in that belief structure is now released.

Sometimes you find yourself having an unusual insight; often it is accompanied by a sense of strangeness, of dislocation, of being lost without familiar beacons. Don't worry! It won't last too long! Your mind will eliminate the thought very quickly and herd you back into your comfort zone. If you're lucky, you'll have a moment when you can explore that feeling; that is a message from your Higher Self, offering you an alternative perspective. Then your mind will rush in with its chatter and push this strange thought away, and you'll forget about it because it doesn't fit into your accepted worldview.

Your mind is terrified of what will happen if you get out of your comfort zone of safe beliefs. It maintains a fierce determination to defend those beliefs, *no matter how illogical*, and releases them only with great difficulty. When you start having unexpected thoughts and perceptions, the last thing it wants is for you to examine them; you might actually make serious changes in your life.

A perfect example is an alcoholic who stops drinking. Surprisingly, the rest of the family, instead of supporting the abstinence, works strenuously (usually tacitly) to force him back to drink, no matter how destructive for everyone. Why? If one person in the family changes, everyone else has to look at their own behavior and attitudes. That means they'd get pulled out of their "safe" world. And they don't want to do that. For them, the familiar dysfunction, though awful, is *safer* than change, and that's what the family will protect. (Family therapy during and after rehab is designed to forestall this outcome.)

Your mind tries hard to enable your dysfunctional behavior. However, when a new idea slides into your belief system, it creates a serious change in your attitudes and beliefs, so that it's hard to remain the same person you were. You maybe forced to confront the ultimate choice: stay and conform, or leave the group and give up your beliefs or new behaviors. That's why your mind, your family, and your friends will try desperately to stop that process from happening. It makes them all too uncomfortable–because you are "different". Your decision may turn your whole life upside down, especially if you persist in your own path.

Self-Image

You form your self-image based on how popular you are, what you believe about yourself, and your attitude toward others and the world.

This self-image affects everything you do, feel, desire, or fear, and it affects your vibrations.

Your self-image has been woven from all your beliefs—usually negative. Every time you are criticized by others or by your mind, or you feel diminished in some way; you reinforce that negative self-image.

Have you had this experience? You call your parents to crow about some major achievement in your life, and they say something like, "Yes, but...your marriage failed," or "...You don't have any children yet." Your self-esteem is completely deflated by their disparaging comments, and your accomplishment is totally invalidated.

You don't have the ability and strength to reject their injurious comments because you define yourself according to your inner image, not your accomplishments. (And your mind proceeds to voice those same criticisms, ad nauseum—which just intensifies your poor self-image. Of course, that shuts you away from your Higher Self because your mind convinces you that you are unworthy of such positive attention.

I have worked with many women who say they're not good enough or not successful enough—in other words, they're not perfect. Their family, employers, and acquaintances, wittingly or unwittingly, perpetuate their feelings of diminishment. When I have directed my clients to go inside their minds, and locate their inner self-image, they have discovered a picture that is way out of date—and way out of balance.

For example, how can women create a healthy internal body image with pictures of thin models assaulting them in all the media? Women striving to match that ideal develop bulimia, anorexia, and other compulsive eating habits, to the detriment of their health and well-being, for they have accepted and internalized that flawed image of themselves as too fat.

Many overweight people see a very thin inner image (and very thin people see a fat image). What better way to make yourself feel worse than by comparing yourself to an ideal that you simply cannot achieve! Not only do you mentally beat yourself up, you overindulge in food because you need to assuage your pain and misery—which continues to feed your negative self-image—and the vicious cycle continues. Every time you do that, energy gets trapped in psychic fat cells.

If your internal image appears worthless and unhappy, then you're going to project worthlessness and sadness. Unless you have done a lot of work on yourself, you don't realize that *rarely* does your inner image bear *any* resemblance to reality. How can you see it clearly when your beliefs about yourself get in the way? Nor can you see anything else because your belief system won't let you.

It's very important to look at what kind of inner image you hold about yourself. Then you can create a new image of yourself, that is no longer idealized or outdated. By doing this simple exercise, you start cracking apart the belief that you are unworthy, and create space for something new and more positive to replace it.

Leora was overweight and depressed, with very low self-esteem (regardless of the fact that she was a highly paid corporate manager). When she looked at her inner image, she saw a very slender woman wearing a black sheath with pearls, and a perfect coiffure, unlike her limp blond mop. "This is the Ice Princess," she said, "very cold and unfeeling. Looking at her makes me feel awful because she's everything I'm not." I asked her to get rid of the picture for exactly that reason and construct a new image of herself as she would like to look in three months. She created an image of herself as somewhat thinner and happier than she really was. From now on, whenever she looked at this new image (not the unlamented Ice Princess), she could make a self-comparison without feeling guilt or shame.

Interestingly, three months later she discovered that she had grown into the image and exactly matched it in attitude, hairstyle, and weight–and it was all accomplished unconsciously.

EXERCISES

Changing Your Inner Image

It's important to do this exercise every few months in order to bring your image up to date.

1. Do the aura cleanout and use your present time wand. Call on your Higher Self for support (very important when facing your own sense of unworthiness abour yourself).
2. Close your eyes, and bring yourself into a private sacred space inside your head. Notice a picture of yourself on one wall.
3. Examine it carefully. What do you see in this picture?
   - Does it show you right now, today? Not ten days ago, not ten weeks ago, not ten years ago–but now?

- How are you dressed? Stylish? Slovenly? In children's clothing? Ugly or designer clothes? Slutty clothes? Do you like what you're wearing?
- What do you look like? What's your hair style? Are you too thin? Too fat? The same?
- Are you holding anything, or are there things in the picture besides you?
- Are there other people in the picture, like your parents, spiritual teacher, etc.? If so, how do they look (gleeful, angry, hurt, judgmental)? What is their attitude toward you? Are they supportive, repressive, controlling?
- How do you *feel*–happy, unhappy, depressed, angry, contented, frustrated, ugly, ashamed, etc.?

4. Take your inner image off the wall and drop it into a handy vat of gold liquid (imagine one in the room with you). No matter how big the picture, the vat is large enough to contain it. Let it soak for a few moments.

5. Take the picture out of the vat. Does it look the same as before? Notice what's different. (There *will* be changes, no matter how subtle. If you don't see or sense them, don't worry. They have still occurred.)

6. Dispose of this picture in some way: Blow it up, tear it up, break it into pieces, burn it, drop it in the ocean, melt it in the vat of gold, throw it into the earth to be recycled, etc.,– whatever feels right to you.

7. Ask your Higher Self to construct a picture of yourself as you wish to be *in three months.* If you're depressed, see yourself as somewhat happier; or if you're sick, see your health improving. If you're overweight, see yourself as a few pounds (5-10) lighter. Your Higher Self will provide the healthiest and most positive picture for you. Hang it on the wall.

8. Cover it with a gold ball of light; then let that gold light expand through your body and aura as well.

9. Say this simple affirmation several times: "I completely accept myself and all my needs, problems, shortcomings, and desires, as I am right now."

This particular affirmation accepts you as you are, and does not make judgments about you. (As you say these words, your mind may come up with its usual comments, negative and positive. Just thank your mind for its comments and continue repeating the affirmation.)

The next exercise will help you remove the judgments you hold about your body. They become easier to remove when the image holding them in place has been removed.

Cleaning Off Body Judgments

This exercise is crucial. You may not realize how you store within you other people's judgments about yourself, your mind, your body, or your self-image until you clean them out. They're like extra baggage you are lugging around. After doing this exercise, who and what you see in the mirror will be without the accretion of judgments and recriminations that have accumulated on you over the years.

1. Clean out your aura and put yourself into present time.
2. Imagine a large vat filled with gold liquid with a spigot at the bottom.
3. Imagine putting a picture of yourself into the barrel, and letting it dissolve into the liquid.
4. Tap the vat with the present time wand, so everything inside is in present time.
5. To remove beliefs about your body:
   a. Ask that all the beliefs that come from your family go away. Open the spigot and let that energy drain into the earth. (You may see it and all the other energies as particular colors. For this exercise, see family energy as **red**.)
   b. Ask that all beliefs about yourself that you got from teachers and spiritual leaders be drained away (**orange energy**).
   c. Pour out all the beliefs you absorbed from friends and relationships (**dark green energy**).
   d. Drain away all the beliefs that came from television, advertising, and other outer sources (**gray energy**).
   e. Whatever remains in the vat belongs strictly to you. If you have very little liquid left, you have been strongly influenced by others. If there is quite a bit, you have already managed to rid yourself of many outside influences.
   f. Once you've drained away the foreign energies, you can shape your image as you would like it.

6. Ask the angels to fill the vat with divine love, happiness, good feelings, and self-love. Imagine that each one of these is a sparkling lovely color.
7. Ask your Higher Self to add acceptance of your body's shape and size as it is without judgments to the liquid. You have created your "self mix." Stir.
8. When you've done all that, imagine climbing into the barrel to soak up these colored energies. Let them be absorbed into your body. For the first time, you are giving your body a new image of itself that is entirely different. You are perfect just the way you are!
9. When you're ready, you can climb out.

Chapter 7
Miscommunication

There are times when your energy seems to be flowing, but somehow it gets scrambled. You think whatever is going on is in the best direction for you—and then things go awry or sideways. It's like your wires got crossed.

In Chapter 9, Who You Attract, you'll see that who and what you attract are completely controlled by your inner wiring and the patterns that have been formed by them. Although the information comes in to your aura/mind/emotional body, it doesn't do what it is supposed to do.

Let me illustrate from couples therapy. When I'm talking to a couple about communication, I show them the little drawing you see below.

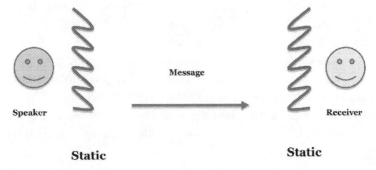

The Speaker, the Receiver, and the Message comprise all communication. Supposedly, when the receiver hears the message, s/he understands clearly what the speaker is saying, and provides an equally-clear response. Alas, communication is rarely that simple. It is, in fact, the major reason that personal and business relationships fail or go haywire. (Over 90% of relationship issues revolve around poor communication.) Why is it so hard to express our message clearly to our listener, and why can't we receive their message clearly?

The answer is simply the other component in the diagram—the "static" between the speaker and receiver. Note that there are two walls of static, one for each member of the communication. Static is made up of beliefs, traumas, experiences, feelings and associationsthat distort any message. I express myself through all of my screens and filters, and you receive that message through all of your screens and filters.

If you're angry at me and I tell you, "I love you," even though you hear the word "love", you interpret it as mockery, or bitterness, or game-playing, or a put-down, not tenderness and affection. Because of that, you *react*, based on all your static—usually with a hostile/angry/upset/hurt response. In turn, the other person *reacts* to your comment—and the fight is on. Sanity has gotten lost in the abyss of miscommunication.

So how can we avoid it? Unfortunately, it's difficult because all those screens and filters fill us. Everything we hear is interpreted (distorted) by our screens (our static). This causes us a lot of misery, whether it is in our inner communication, inner perceptions and judgements, or outer communication with others. The only way to lose those distortions is to lose those screens.

Here's a simple and common example: Someone compliments you on a nice outfit, and you reply, "That old outfit? Nah, this isn't so good." You aren't just denying what they say; you are expressing your sense of low self worth. (The right answer is, "Thank you.")

Here's another example from couples therapy. Occasionally, I might compliment one of them: "Your dress looks very nice on you." She says, "Thank you," and acts very pleased with me. He turns to her and, quite irritated, says, "I compliment you all the time!" She responds, "You're just saying those things because you're married to me, not because you mean them." Now, he looks pretty outraged. "I DO mean it!" he protests. She replies, "No, you don't."

This is static. For this woman, her filter says, "I will not believe anything nice that you (or anyone close to me) says about me."

If you think that isn't a common scenario, not only with couples, but with family and friends, you would be completely wrong. I am amazed at how often people will take compliments from strangers but not the near-and-dear.

There are many reasons for that, such as that your loved ones have their own agendas: They're playing games with you because they really know how worthless a person you are, and they can't *really* mean such a compliment; so there has to be some other reason for their saying it.

(That is why I spend a good amount, teaching couples how to accept compliments from each other.)

What happens is that you are *twisting* the message. Your screens filter out the good message and leave the negative. The internal wiring in your brain, your mental body, needs to be dismantled, and something more positive put in to replace it.

One of the simplest ways to start is through affirmations. Affirmations are simple positive statements: I am happy. I look good today. I like myself. But they are explosively powerful!

When you say an affirmation, what happens is that everything inside of you that is mis-wired or out of alignment with those statements is going to try **very, very hard** to negate *everything* you say by actively proving the opposite of what the affirmation says. A sentence like "I look good today" will cause you to get feedback that says "You're ugly"–both from your inner negative wiring in the form of criticism, and from the world outside you. The plan is for you to give up saying the affirmation. Don't! Even though you want to. That's the programming inside you that needs to be removed so the positive affirmation can rewire your system.

It's not easy to find that wiring unless you use affirmations–which show exactly where you are warped. It's very important to do affirmations every day.

If you are going to work on healing your past, you must confront all of these filters and screens and bad wiring.

EXERCISES

Rainbow Run

You are going to run rainbow light through your body. This is very good when you are feeling very agitated and upset, and especially, when you feel negated. The reason I like a rainbow is that it covers the whole spectrum of energies in all chakras because most issues have hooks or wiring in more than one of the chakras. That means one issue gets cleaned out in all areas. Think of shame. You can feel shame in your first chakra (survival), second (sex/emotions), third (manipulation), fourth (unworthiness), and fifth (speech–shamed by telling truth or fear of speaking your truth). The rainbow works on every chakra.

1. Sit down and ground yourself. Put yourself into present time.

2. Ask for a beam of sunlight to come down from the sun. Above your head, there is a prism that splits the sunlight into the seven colors. No matter what kind of weather is out there, the sun will always be able to send a beam of light through all the clouds into the prism above your head.

3. Let the rainbow flow into your head, down your spine, torso, legs and into the earth, and down your arms and hands. It's like you're taking a shower from the inside.

4. As you run this inner shower, say aloud, "I am releasing my anger/agitation/frustration/hurt/shame (or whatever emotion you are feeling)." Speaking your words aloud is very important.

5. As you express whatever emotion you are feeling, this cleanout takes away the emotion, it cleanses the filter or screen it's attached to.

6. Imagine this rainbow of colors sinking into all of your cells, where it scrubs out the negativity that is being triggered.

7. Keep saying, "I am releasing my fear/my anger/my anxiety" etc., and let the rainbow pull all of that negative wiring out of you and down into the earth.

8. Imagine that the colors scrubbing the neurons inside your brain that are being fired/triggered by your words.

9. Then allow the rainbow of light to flow down from the brain to each of the chakras and into the earth.

10. If you don't know what you're feeling, just say, "Whatever emotion I'm feeling, let that be removed from my mind and my body by the rainbow of light." Then run the rainbow through you. That's all you need to do to remove the energies.

11. Keep breathing.

12. After 5-10 minutes of this, let the colors drain out of you.

13. Fill yourself with gold light to fill up the areas inside you that were emptied and cleansed by the rainbow.

Affirmations

Affirmations are positive statements that go right into your unconscious—and that creates powerful change. Because they go into your subconscious, they MUST be positive. Examples are: I like myself. I am happy. I make lots of money. I have a great, loving relationship with my spouse. I feel great.

Do NOT use any negatives, such as not, never, don't, won't. This is why: your subconscious functions with positives. If you say, "I'm not miserable," your subconscious will strip away the negative word ("not"). So what's left? "I'm miserable." That's what your subconscious will make sure happens.

1. Say each affirmation five times in each chakra (that's 35 times altogether).
2. Afterward, you have a choice of doing either of the following
   a. Call on Archangel Michael to remove all the energies that have been activated by those affirmations.
   b. Run violet energy through your body to remove the wiring that has been activated by those affirmations.
3. Fill yourself with gold light to fill all those areas that have had their warped wiring removed.

CHAPTER 8
EMOTIONAL SELF

The symbol of the emotional body is the Inner Child—who is very immature, impulsive, reactive, sensitive—everything your "rational" mind is not. She/he lives in a world shaped by fear of some kind—fear of mistreatment or abuse, abandonment, shame, rage, neglect, or other emotions. And so do you—because your Child's needs drive your adult behavior and is hard to contain or "reason with" when out of control. Working with your emotional body means working with childhood issues. By following your feelings down into your body, you'll find your Inner Child.

All the real traumas you've lived through get triggered every time something similar happens in your adult life—like being yelled at by a spouse, or feeling abandoned by your lover. With each "charged" memory, the shame, fear, humiliation, rage, abandonment, loss, and/or helplessness that you felt in the past get activated in your emotional body; moreover, it resonates with other similar events, in your past, so its effects become cumulative. That will continue until you can release its power. The abuse has become hard-wired in you.

The level of fear in your emotional body indicates the strength of the trauma embedded in your body, and the obstacles that must be overcome for healing to occur.

If you are afraid of authority figures because you had a rage-aholic father, releasing this childhood trauma from your emotional body means you are no longer controlled by that same kind of overwhelming terror as an adult.

Before embarking on any inner work, you must remember that the person reliving this experience is your Inner Child, *not you, the adult.* She made decisions about herself, her self-worth, and her lovability, based on being abused, neglected, emotionally smothered, shamed, or hurt. You, the adult, may get angry at your Child for her decisions, but, please remember, she chose *survival*. It might help for you to take a moment to forgive her for what she endured so that **you** could stay alive long enough to grow up.

Childhood traumas are not simple memories; they are as alive now as when they occurred. It's the difference between a photo and a video. A photo is neutral; a video shows the actual event, which provokes powerful emotional reactions. Your Inner Child is trapped in his own videos of emotional and physical abuse and needs to be released from them.

Healing yourself means breaking free of the spider web of the past and turning the traumas (videos) turn into memories (photo album). To do that, you must confront the childhood experiences in your inner world and help the Inner Child's release his feelings.

Finding A Memory

You need inner resources like your Higher Self or a guardian angel to accompany you during this process. They help you negotiate the passage through your trauma with greater ease. Your Higher Self will give you *only as strong a memory as you can safely handle emotionally.*

I cannot emphasize enough that you rely on your Higher Self's wisdom! It knows how much emotional pain you can handle and how to protect you. In other words, don't do your work without inner support! You don't want to become overwhelmed by whatever comes up. If you open yourself up without that precaution, you might crumble from the onslaught of the experience, not only during the process, but in the weeks to follow.

How do you find an appropriate memory?

1. Think of moments in your childhood or early teenage years. Then pay attention to any sensations in your physical body. You may feel something in your stomach, heart, throat, eyes–either emotional in tone (sad, angry, hurt) or physical (tightness, squeezing, fluttery, heaviness, or stopped, shallow, or fast breathing). Or you may notice nothing. The absence of feeling, or numbness, is your body's mechanism for disguising severe pain. Notice where in your body you feel this deadness. If you can detect nothing, and that often happens when starting this kind of work, it simply means your body is trying to protect you.

2. If you recall where you felt bodily pain when you did the alignment exercise in Chapter 5, start there. (Repeat the

exercise again to reacquaint yourself with these blocks, if necessary.)

3. Say the sentence, "*I deserve love*" twice. "*I deserve love*" carries an enormous emotional wallop. You'll hear at least one voice (or several) in your mind disagreeing (loudly) with that statement, and usually a concurrent physical or emotional reaction–including, perhaps, going numb.

By this time, you should be used to the mind's ongoing commentary. Throughout the whole process, in fact, count on those mental voices continuing to make comments, usually negative. Just acknowledge them by saying, "Thank you" and return to your process. Otherwise, they'll get more strident, like a persistent child tugging on your leg for attention. Once acknowledged, they will subside, or reduce their volume. These voices are terrified you will make changes–and where will they be?

Transforming a Memory

Whenever you transform past events, several things happen:

- You transform traumas into simple memories and free up the trapped energy.
- You begin to reempower yourself because you no longer are at the mercy of the past.
- You release your suppressed anger, and reclaim any unacceptable emotions (i.e., whatever was unacceptable in your family).
- You dismantle the old traumatic neuron pathways in your brain and create new loving and healing pathways.
- You create a space inside yourself to accept love and joy.

During this process, you may cry, yell, or just remain silent. The more you feel, the stronger your release. Even if you treat the process as an intellectual exercise and experience little emotion, merely *doing* it lets your body know that you are open to self-transformation. After awhile, the emotions will begin pour out because your child will feel safe enough to out her or his long-suppressed feelings. Indeed, your Inner Child may not trust you enough to participate in this work at first, though by the second or third attempt, s/he'll participate because you have shown that you are serious about healing yourself.

Fiona related a horrific incident of her stepfather hurting her pet. She had worked on this issue with many therapists over many years, but the trauma was still alive in her. When we went back to the memory, she started to regress, but I told her to separate from her Inner Child and remain the adult. As the adult, she immediately stopped her stepfather from his abuse and then sent him off for punishment, while her Higher Self comforted her Child. When she came back into the room, she reported incredible body sensations of lightness and relief. And weeks later she got her first pet since childhood.

What goes on during the process?

Real transformation. That is the goal of this exercise–not to relive the trauma, but to *resolve* it. Once and for all.

By stepping into child Fiona's scenario, the adult stopped reliving the memory with all its concomitant horror, and made conscious and firm choices to change the story line. As she did so, she felt immediate physical reactions (cold chills) that indicated that something really different was happening.

Afterward, she commented that, no matter what we did to stop the abuse inside her, it didn't change the reality of its happening. And she was right. The horrific event DID occur–years earlier. But–and this is what I want to emphasize–that experience was *still alive in her*, still happening, over and over, year after year. It was not in the past, in her "inner reality", until she and I put it there. Then, and only then, did it become merely a photo in her album of life.

This is what happens when you change your inner reality:

1. Healing the event not only releases it in both your physical and emotional bodies, it raises your vibration, as the energy trapped by the trauma has been freed up for you to have now.
2. It creates physiological change in your brain. When you disrupt a strong memory by changing it, you disrupt the old neural pathway in your brain. Your neurons fire in different patterns and create a new neural pathway that no longer contains that trauma. You also have a new memory of self-empowerment.
3. Once the emotional abscess has been drained, you have created a space to fill up with new life and vitality–and love and forgiveness.

Anger

Sooner or later, you will start feeling anger–legitimate, overwhelming rage that you have stuffed inside yourself. The more traumatized the child, the greater the suppressed rage that needs to be expressed by you (no matter what you the adult would like). For example, sexually-abused children were betrayed on two levels–first, physically, and second, emotionally–because the adult both manipulated the child into believing he or she was the cause of the incest, and violated the adult/parental role.

The Inner Child must be allowed to express his feelings, no matter what they are, and he needs to feel accepted and loved while doing so. Let your Child kick, yell, pound a pillow (pretending it's the abuser) until he is done. Regardless of how horrified you may feel as an adult about his rage, your disapproval of this *justifiable* anger is just as destructive as your parent's abuse. Adult reason and civility have no reality for the Child. He must let his primal emotions out, so they can be released from *YOU!*

If you cannot accept your Child's anger, your Higher Self and the angels can. This is where the angelic presence is very helpful. Angels are filled with an enormous, inexhaustible source of love. They love your Inner Child without judgment or conditions. All you have to do is accept it. Even though you the adult may have trouble accepting angelic love, your Child won't–not from an angel. Children trust angels.

EXCERCISE

Releasing a Childhood Trauma

You might want to do this exercise with a friend who can read the steps and the suggestions while you are doing the process. Even if you do it alone, and you need to consult the book as to what comes next, opening your eyes and reading the information and then going back inside will not hinder your work. Really!

Resources: Two pillows, or one pillow and one stuffed animal.

1. Find a quiet place to do this work. You don't want to be disturbed. Have your pillows/stuffed animal handy. Do the aura cleanout and use the present time wand.
2. Call in your Higher Self or guardian angel. They will be there to support you. You should not be alone during this process. Imagine them putting their hands on your shoulders or holding your hand.
3. Choose a memory. (Don't pick something deeply upsetting like sexual abuse the first time, just an incident that gives you an uncomfortable buzz.)

4. If you don't have one readily available you can do the following:
    a. Say *"I deserve love,"* twice. It will cause a reaction inside you. Then ask your Higher Self to bring up the memory of one time you experienced that uncomfortable feeling in your childhood.
    b. Imagine there's a large suitcase, and inside it are your painful memories. Reach inside and grab one.
    c. Repeat the alignment exercise in Chapter 5.
5. Close your eyes and imagine watching your chosen incident unfold on your inner television. *Don't fall into the memory. Just watch!* Being the observer releases you from the grip of extremely painful emotions, so it becomes merely a TV show.
    a. If the incident is difficult to watch, breathe slowly and deeply (at times like this, people either freeze or panic). That's why the first few times you do this work, you don't want to watch a major trauma.
    b. If you start to regress into the Child, with all the Child's emotions, ask your Higher Self or angels to help pull you back into the adult watching the story on the TV; by doing so, you will be able to access your adult resources, and not get swept up in the Child's fear.
    c. So how do you dissociate?
        1. Freeze the action on the screen (use the remote to touch Pause). This gives you some perspective.
        2. Take some deep slow breaths, and open your eyes to reorient yourself into the present. Then go back into the memory.
        3. Ask your Higher Self to take over and keep you safe.
6. Take a pillow and ask that all the feelings you are having be drained into the pillow. Then put the pillow aside.
7. As soon as the parent starts the abuse, ask your Higher Self and angels to enter the scene. Now, instead of the parent and child alone, there's a parent, a child, adult you, your Higher Self, and/or angels. Notice the parent's (or abuser's) reaction;

he or she *will* react to this sudden audience—their kind of abuse doesn't like spectators.

8. Stop the action. If you feel strong enough yourself, YOU can stop the parent with the support of your higher beings. Otherwise, let them do it. *For the first time, the child is no longer alone, defenseless or abandoned. She or he has been rescued from an abuser.*

9. At this point your instinct might be to remove the Inner Child from the abusive situation rather than cuddle her. Don't. If you do, the abuse will remain stuck in your body.

10. Ask your Higher Self to hold and comfort your Inner Child. Actually holding a tangible soft object (stuffed animal or pillow) in your physical arms can trigger an enormous release in your emotional body (like anger or tears). Let your Higher Self reassure your child that she is no longer alone, that she is protected by the Higher Self and the angels, and that no one will hurt her.

11. If the Child wants to hit and scream at the parent, you can pound on a pillow until your Child feels complete or drained (not the pillow you are holding!).

12. Ask the Child where he/she wants to send the parent for reeducation or punishment. (Reeducation means sending them to a place where they can learn to be better parents; punishment is punishment.) Your Child may feel one or two emotions—fury at the parent, terror at being abandoned, or both at the same time. Kids normally don't want to hurt their parents or get rid of them, no matter how abusive they've been, since the kids live in constant dread of being abandoned.

13. Let the Child decide what retribution is appropriate. Be aware that your adult ideas and your Child's ideas are usually wildly different.

14. Call on the angels to haul off the abuser to the place of parental re-education or punishment. No matter how strong the abuser is, he/she is no match for the power of an angel or two. Watch as two (or more) of them haul them off by the arms (and legs).

15. Ask the angels to remove the trapped energy of that experience from your body. Imagine them opening a closet inside the

area that hurts and sucking out all of the pain and emotions trapped in the memory, removed from your space forever.

16. Then let them spread divine love into that closet (you can visualize it like golden fog, or just a sparkly sensation). You don't have to do any work or even imagine it; it just happens. Allow it to fill the cells of your whole body. Letting divine love flow through you alters your brain, chips away at your mind's belief system, releases the trauma from your emotional body, and frees up your energy.

17. When you're finished, open your eyes.

18. Thank your Higher Self (or angels) for helping and guiding the process.

You might notice nothing at the moment, but later on you may have an emotional reaction or a sense of release. Think of it like pieces of an intricate hand puzzle clicking into alignment. The more work you do, the more opportunity for letting go of more blocks.

The effect is cumulative.

CHAPTER 9
WHO YOU ATTRACT

Are you looking for your soulmate? (Lots of us are.)

Where is s/he?

How can you attract him/her?

That is a most pertinent question—because attracting your soulmate is completely dependent on things beyond your conscious control. Enough pop psychology books have been written about bad relationships. Ultimately, they boil down to: *You attract what you know* (parents), and this attraction is closely linked to your childhood *survival*.

The patterns and beliefs and views that led you to a particular partner were stamped into your psyche by the primary adult relationship in your life—that of your parents. This unconscious—but entirely influential—program has governed your choice of adult partner.

Instead of choosing someone who is "perfect" for your *soul*, your inner programming looks for someone that matches what *it wants*. That means "somebody who I can be codependent with," or "somebody who I can ignore but who will take care of my needs." "And, by the way, since my mother/father drank, I will only be interested in an alcoholic or other kind of addict, as well." If you had a childhood with a violent father and compliant mother, unluckily, you're apt to be either violent, and marry someone who tolerates that behavior, or be compliant with a violent or rageaholic partner.

> *Nina says all she has to do is go to a party, and the only man who appeals to her turns out to be the one alcoholic—just like her father. (This is a frighteningly common occurrence for many of us.)*

Have you had this experience? Each time you get involved with a new partner, you're in ecstasy because you believe you're found your perfect lover. *This time* this person is special, i.e., not like your parents. Then about four to six months later, the rosy glasses slip off your eyes, and you can see your partner more clearly–and the honeymoon's over–they have transformed instantly from a prince to a toad. You then wonder to yourself whether you're in love with this person any more, but since you're lying next to him/her, you two are either going to accept each other's flaws and make this relationship work, or you are going to split up.

If you move on, you will likely repeat the whole process with the same result. Over and over again. Afterward, you say to your friends in dismay, "Why do I keep attracting these some people? What is wrong with me?" They can only sigh. (However, they're no better because they do the same thing as well. It's just easier to recognize when someone else makes mistakes, not you.) You don't realize that your choice of partner is completely predictable–as well as the progress of your relationship.

Even though your *conscious* mind may try to choose a lover *rationally*, your inner programming (based on your parents' relationship) governs ALL of your choices, *no matter what you say you want*. It also guarantees that the kind of relationship you form with your lover will recreate the same set of circumstances you had as a child (or its exact opposite), except that now you're an adult. You have created a self-fulfilling prophecy.

What's going on? Your mental screens filter out candidates according to familiarity with your parents. You can *consciously* state your preference for one kind of person, but an unconscious part inside you (the Inner Child) has a different set of criteria for its choice–primarily involving its personal safety. (Does this begin to sound familiar?)

All of your relationships have a survival quality to them. As a child you knew you could only survive by acting in a certain way to get your needs met (whether it was love or attention) or to avoid pain, hurt, or shame. Now, as an adult, struggling to make adult choices, you're still governed by your Inner Child's need for safety. That plays the critical role in your choice of partner.

A familiar relationship, healthy or not, makes you feel safer because you know how to function in that environment. That means you're more apt to remain in an abusive relationship than leave because you know what's expected of you–no matter how painful it may be (unless you've done some serious work on changing your patterns). It's "the devil you know...."

Carlyle, a kind and gentle man, met Aileen and fell in love. She had come out of a long-term abusive marriage. He did everything he could to let her know how much he loved her, but after a few months, she broke it off because, she said, she couldn't trust him not to turn into the same kind of violent man as her ex.

That is a perfect example of being controlled by your programming. Aileen just could not even conceive of being involved with someone other than the kind of person she knew.

Now, you don't have to take on all the responsibility for your relationship; you're only half of the problem. If you have your own limited certain attraction program, your partner has a similar one, with their own survival criteria.

Both of you are equally responsible for choosing each other.

Reprogramming Yourself

Your inner programming limits you to only one or even two perspectives—if you're lucky. When you begin to remove your internal screens, negative energies, and patterns from your space, your horizon expands to a much more multi-dimensional view.

It's like you were looking through a keyhole, and then you opened the door and discovered a picture window. Even if you choose to shut the door, you know there exists a larger vista, whether you want to ignore it or not.

As you transform, bit by bit, your old patterns and beliefs, you'll find yourself making new choices about the kinds of relationships you want in your life—with friends, and more particularly, with lovers. When that begins to happen, the people around you (friends/family/partner) will do everything they can to disrupt the process and force you back into your old safe familiar (dysfunctional and unsatisfying) patterns.

That will present you with a choice: Should you take care of them—or you? Here are three options for you:

1) You choose to continue healing, and they accept the new you and change themselves;

2) You accede to their pressure and revert to your old behavior; or

3) You split up.

This is a huge issue when you begin to work on yourself, and your partner does not. As you start dismantling your inner structure, and you decide not to tolerate dysfunctional interactions any longer, your relationship will come under severe strain and can easily fracture. Hopefully, as the patterns that originally attracted you to your partner disappear, something else remains in your relationship—the love, affection, respect you have for each other—along with your partner's willingness to change as well, so you both can become a stronger couple. (Couples counseling is *strongly* recommended at that juncture.)

Unfortunately, the differences between you two may become insurmountable, until you split up. Even if you do revert to behavior #2, you're still likely to split up sooner or later because it's very difficult to turn back into your old self without serious personal psychological damage. Then you're left looking for a new relationship, hoping to create something different the next time.

Using your present time wand to clean out of your aura (ideally, every day) will remove whatever has been stirred up inside you. That means whenever an old pattern is suddenly activated, such as the one that says you can only be involved with certain types of people, you can keep releasing its energy until it is removed.

One way to do that is by asking yourself, "What do I get from attracting this person into my life?" Asking that question allows you to examine your motives—which usually have safety as a basis. When you can recognize the price you paid for being with the partner you chose, you can begin to consider other choices..

As long as you continue to work on yourself, your subsequent relationships will be different.

Releasing the Rigid Program

Taking the steps required to change means replacing your inner attraction program, which is hardwired inside your brain and in your chakras. The energy circuits of the lower chakras are gummed up by old programming about love. (The following chart illustrates that programming.)

1st Chakra Love	=	Survival
2nd Chakra Love	=	Sex
3rd Chakra Love	=	Power/manipulation
4th Chakra Love	=	With conditions

You need to reconfigure your chakras to attract a new vibration.

Your first chakra, at the tailbone, governs survival of all kinds. Since anything you do may affect your physical survival, your first chakra is always activated, even if at a very low level. That means a love relationship is assessed according to how *safe* you will be.

Your second chakra (three inches above your groin) governs sexuality. Here is the sexual energy that equates love with sex (for example, women as sex *objects*, not as sex *partners*). That kind of demeaning energy needs to be eliminated. That doesn't mean getting rid of *sexuality* or the joy of sex, just the program that dehumanizes or debases you, or limits the possibilities of pleasure to certain acceptable behaviors.

Energies to be removed from your third chakra at the solar plexus are power over others or you. Power is fine, but not when used to control or dominate or manipulate of you or your partner. It can either be naked (through emotions like anger) or covert (as in playing the victim or using guilt to get what you want).

Finally, love resides in your fourth chakra, your heart. As a child, you learned two "truths":

1. There is only a finite (and small) amount of love in the world.
2. You could have love with certain usually *unspoken* conditions ("I can have love when its given to me with a slap on the side of the head, or when I'm criticized, or when my partner (parent) approves, or when I perform the right role"). And if you didn't toe that line, you didn't deserve love.

Both of those beliefs are **not true**. If you are feeling unloved and unworthy, or if you have been programmed not to accept love, it's very difficult to perceive it when it's there. These two very destructive messages need to be removed from your heart chakra and replaced by the message that love is inexhaustible and flowing–and you always deserve it.

Changing the Attraction Template

In each chakra is an Attraction Template created by you many years ago. I visualize it as similar to a player piano roll. The roll is already prepunched so the piano can only play certain keys–and nothing else.

It is exactly the same with your Attraction Template. It doesn't matter what you *think* you want; **you can't change the program**. It's already been set up to allow in only somebody who matches that prearranged configuration (unless you've done a lot of work on yourself).

A limited template

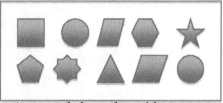

An expanded template with many different options

Note in the two pictures how one template has only two shapes, whereas the other has at least ten distinctly different shapes, and is at least twice the size of the other template. A *limited template* only lets in those energies that match its three paltry shapes—and it's small. An *expanded template* is larger, and has a lot more options (choices) available.

It's time to change or retire the old limited template in each chakra, so it looks like the expanded template. Then you unplug all the cords and wires hooked into the template, so you can release all the links you have with all of your partners, and with your parents—where the programs came from.

You may suddenly perceive some strange and even uncomfortable sensations, like unease, abandonment or fear. Don't worry; it takes some time to get used to the idea that you are no longer controlled by other people's programs.

It you feel you want to plug the cords back in after you do this exercise, you will be able if you want to—but, frankly, once they're gone, it's far healthier for you to keep them out. The only place you should have any cords connecting you to other people is from your heart chakra—and those are of pure love.

The next step is to actually remove the template from your each chakra, clean it off, and bring it into present time. Then you can create another one altogether.

Should you opt to retain your old template, it simply means you are content to make changes at a more deliberate pace. However, I have found, over and over again, that it is best to create a new template than use the old one, with its old energies and stuck patterns.

In effect, you are creating something brand new inside yourself, which will trigger all sorts of changes in your attitudes, behaviors, and beliefs. When you let go of these old limiting programs, your life and your connection with your partner will shift; the underpinnings of your old relationship no longer exist, so you can create new ones that reflect the new improved you. That's proof that your work is making a difference.

Doing this exercise means that you are no longer wired for your old relationships. That doesn't mean that you *instantly* start attracting someone different. After all, you still have the programming in other places–like your mental body's screens, and your aura. But you'll have a harder time clinging to those beliefs and patterns because the root (template) is no longer there. You can begin to make other less damaging choices for your life.

What You Attract

Not only do you attract what you know; you also attract what is *complementary* to what's inside of you. It's not inherent in you, but it *enhances* what's going on inside of you. Unlike your template, which is a predisposition to attract something, it is more like a satellite dish, which is collecting information and vibrations from around you to pass on to your brain and any appropriate chakra. It is programmed to give you certain experiences, at different times of your life, good and bad.

I don't want to take away your karmic or life lessons you need to have, but why make your life so miserable? I would prefer that you have lessons learned with ease, and grace, and healing. We need to change the Dish's program so that what you get is not *bad* stuff but the *right* stuff.

EXERCISES

Rewiring Your Attraction Template

You can use this exercise for ANY issue–such as success, poverty, prosperity, self-esteem, or fear.

We will be working with several chakras, which are connected in some way with your issue (see the chart up above).

1. Get yourself comfortable. Do the cleanout exercises and the present time wand. Close your eyes, and call in your Higher Self.
2. Imagine stepping onto an escalator that takes you and your Higher Self down to your heart.
3. Step off the escalator and look around. Don't expect to see the actual physical beating heart; what you see in your chakra is

completely symbolic. Ask your Higher Self to find the love Attraction Template.

4. Reach out and unplug any cords attached to that template. If you do not see them, imagine that you are unplugging them anyway. Say to yourself, "I am pulling all the cords out of the template and sending them back to whomever they belong (parents, lovers, friends)." You can imagine them zipping off, like a vacuum's retractable cord.

5. Tap the template with your present time wand to bring it into present time. (I guarantee this template is about as far from present time as you are from the moon.) You might notice an instant change, either in the image or in your heart. Then pry it off the wall and drop it into a convenient vat of gold liquid be disposed of. If you need help to remove it, call on your Higher Self or the angels.

6. If there are other pieces of hardware in your chakra that kept your template bolted to the wall, remove them as well, and throw them into the vat; they belong to your old way of thinking.

7. This template is linked to the brain's limbic system (this is the area of the brain that governs emotions) by a large cable. You may see or simply sense the cable. Ask your Higher Self to send a gold ball of light up the cable to the limbic system in the middle of your head. As the ball touches the cable, it dissolves both the cable and any old programming attached to it.

8. Ask your Higher Self to create a new template that reflects the new You.

9. Hang that template on the wall.

10. Run a new golden cord from your template up to the limbic system.

11. Ask the angels to flood the chakra, the cord, and the brain with love.

12. When you're finished, open your eyes.

13. When you repeat this exercise for other chakra:
    a. For the second and third chakras, your cable will go to the limbic system.
    b. For the first chakra, which is associated with survival, the cord goes to your reptilian brain (medulla).

Changing Your Satellite Signal

1. Get yourself comfortable. Do the cleanout exercises and the present time wand. Close your eyes, and call in your Higher Self.
2. At the top of your head and a little bit to the front is your satellite dish.
3. Tap it with your present time wand. You might notice it change shape, color, etc., and you might get an emotional reaction from it.
4. At the bottom in the back is a little door. Open that door and remove the program. Think of it like a computer motherboard, with all its wiring. Tap it with the present time wand to make sure it all comes out.
5. Ask your Higher Self to put in a different program—one that is going to give you positive, healing lessons, so that what you attract is healing and transforming, and not filled with suffering.
6. Send the old program into the earth to be recycled.
7. Close the door, and come back.

CHAPTER 10
FROZEN MOMENTS

If you could imagine your life as a road down which you have been journeying, what would it look like? Take a moment now to close your eyes and visualize your road and its surroundings.

What is your terrain like? How straight is your road? What's coming up ahead? You might find yourself teetering on a twisted, steep footpath on the side of a craggy mountain, or strolling down a pleasant garden lane, or perhaps trudging through a parched desert landscape. Those images you see around your road symbolize the kind of life you've chosen to live.

If you could soar above your road, so you can see it all the way back to its origin, you'd notice how sometimes your road took strange jogs, or barriers or craters or fissures that forced you to move in another direction altogether. Such places are pivot points–events that caused massive and profound changes in your life. How we dealt with them determined our future. Sometimes they were beneficial, though often they indicate disasters that produced devastating consequences, leaving you an emotional and psychic wreck.

Examples of such devastating pivotal moments might be sexual abuse, rape, the death of someone close to you, divorce, major illness, combat experiences, etc. Every one of us probably can recall at least one or two extremely painful pivotal moments in our ives. Today, we label the psychological effects of these disasters as post-traumatic stress disorder (PTSD), and we know they color everything we do, even years after the event. For example, even after so many years, World War II vets still have flashbacks to their battle experiences.

The incredible shock of these serious blows to our system may cause us to change our nature in some profound way. I call these jolts "frozen moments."

When Phyllida was a sophomore in college, she was date-raped—and it shattered her life. She had planned on pursuing singing as a career until the rape—which she blamed herself for. After that, she found she could no longer perform in public. She withdrew into herself, becoming quiet and self-effacing. Twenty years later she was deeply depressed, very unhappy about her job, miserable in her marriage, and wishing she were dead. The rape and the guilt had so overwhelmed her psyche that everything subsequently was a direct result of it. It had become the single defining moment of her life.

The result of such a frozen moment is that it stunts our emotional growth, and we often fall into different, often less-healthy patterns, like addiction, to escape from the trauma and concomitant pain. A frozen moment cuts us off from our potential in a markedly dramatic way. Because of the rape, Phyllida literally choked off her gift of song, believing she was unworthy of it. Though she created a functional adulthood, her joy and her life force were inaccessible.

People can experience frozen moments from local, national, or international events. For many baby boomers, it was President Kennedy's assassination; for others, 9/11. Both of those horrific moments changed the American psyche.

How can you recognize a frozen moment? It has several characteristics:

- It changes your life in some serious way, so that your life veers off in a direction far different from the one you planned. War creates its own set of frozen moments. Soldiers who served in the Vietnam War found their lives markedly and profoundly changed; and many of them still suffer severe post-traumatic stress—as do the veterans of the Iraq and Afghanistan wars—exhibited by addiction, homelessness, uncontrollable anger, and broken marriages.
- It controls your life, whether or not you speak of it, or even recall it. Many sexual abuse victims who have suppressed memories of their abuse often end up in the sex trade (even if they cannot remember the abuse, which is very common for sexual abuse victims). There is a direct correlation between sexual abuse and their chosen careers.
- It is intensely alive in the present moment. If the frozen moment is not personally shameful (like sexual abuse), you

bring it up in conversation (like a death, divorce, catastrophe, etc.), over and over again, like a mantra. Your hope is that, by talking about it a lot, you will either come to terms with it, or diminish its impact. (This is a tenet of psychotherapy–that talking about something enough will reduce its power–but it just dulls the pain.) Instead, you measure yourself according to that experience: "If X hadn't happened, I would have been Y." or "If X hadn't happened, I could have done Y." Or "Since X happened, I can never be/do/have Y because I'm no good/ I'm helpless/I'm to blame." Messages like that compound the guilt.

- You are no longer able to deal with things that you could handle before the event. Even years later, that emotional ability is still missing. It's like having a stroke and regaining only partial use of a limb–you cope, but not nearly as well as before.
- A frozen moment prevents you from living up to your potential.

For your own psychological and spiritual healing, that frozen moment must be released from you.

Until recently, people suffered from their experiences in silence. Now that we know much more about the effects of such traumas, therapy and support groups can help people work through their painful issue. You no longer have suffer post-traumatic stress forever, or by yourself. Between therapy, and a rape support group, Phyllida completely transformed herself. One of the keys to her healing was finally accepting that she was *not to blame* for the rape. Only then, when she stopped blaming herself, could she begin to heal. Eventually, she began to perform in amateur theatricals.

In determining how your frozen moment has affected your life, it is important to consider the following questions. (Do not worry if you cannot come up with answers at first, particularly for something like sexual abuse. You have suppressed those memories for your own survival.)

- What incident(s) in your life do you talk about or reference over and over again? Ask friends for help if you are not sure. They'll know!
- What did you give up after you experienced your frozen moment? It may be a career, family, a relationship, a belief system, trust in self/others/godhood.

- What "bitter lesson" did you learn from the experience? Usually, it's something for which you judge yourself harshly—like Phyllida blaming herself for her rape—or blaming yourself for being molested as a child by an adult who told you that your behavior or looks were the reason for the molestation.

- What has been the price of your loss? In other words, what would your life have been like if that had not occurred? Maybe it happened early enough in your life that you don't know, but most of the time you have some sense of how your life would have gone.

- Are you willing to resolve your frozen moment? (You'd be surprised how many people are *not* willing because they don't have to take responsibility for changing their lives.)

When you decide to deal with the frozen moment and its impact on your life, you may need to pry open a part of yourself that has been sealed off for years, and access the emotions, feelings, and abilities you cut off. That can be terrifying, but if you look at the process from the perspective of healing your pain, you can release the trauma and reclaim lost parts of yourself.

Doing this work requires you to go back and reclaim that frozen part of yourself. In many cases, that means removing the abuser from your energy field and reformulating your present life (see Chapter 8).

This exercise will give you an idea of how ready you are to deal with your frozen moment by "seeing" the box that holds the event. To be able to see it clearly, and not be overwhelmed by its memories, the box needs to be put into present time to release the energy trapped inside it. Even looking at the Frozen Moment Box can be intimidating.

Then, if you feel daring, open the box and remove as much of your energy as you can handle. Of course, it's not just whether you are able to take out any energy—but whether you can even *open* the box. Most people cannot take anything out of the box the first time. Just seeing the box in present time can trigger an enormous emotional reaction. This is the first time that you are actually confronting a shattering experience—no matter how mildly.

EXERCISE

The Frozen Moment Box

1. Close your eyes and do your energy cleanout. Hold on to the present time wand; you'll need it for this exercise.

2. Call in your Higher Self and at least one angel.
3. Ask to imagine your Frozen Moment Box. Your box may be of any size, shape, texture, material, or color.
4. Observe the box. How do you feel? Are you angry? Sad? Happy? Terrified?
5. Take a few deep breaths, and ask the angels to bathe you and the box in sparkling gold love energy.
6. Tap the box with the present time wand several times.
7. If you feel capable of doing so, open the box. Inside is all of the energy from that experience that has been locked away.
8. If you don't feel capable of opening the box yourself, but you do want it opened, ask your Higher Self to do it for you. Notice how you feel as the box is opened.
9. Take a gold dipper. Reach in and scoop out some of your locked-away essence. What does it feel like to do that?
10. Look at what's inside the dipper. Is it a liquid or an object? If it's liquid, pour it over your head and let it be absorbed into you. If you see an object, put it into your heart. You probably will feel some kind of emotion—perhaps strong, perhaps not. This is the first step toward reclaiming who you were.
11. Repeat Steps 9 and 10 as long as you feel capable of doing so. Remember to go slowly. You're bring back a lot of energy into your space and your physical body needs to adjust, so you won't overwhelm it (i.e., get sick).

To further continue healing your frozen moment, I suggest three avenues to pursue:

1. Repeat this exercise and take more of your essence back.
2. Find a support group.
3. Go to therapy, particularly someone who works with energy programs like EFT (Emotional Field Therapy). The combination of a trained professional and a support group with similar issues is quite powerful. Combined with this exercise, they will help you become the wonderful person you were before you frozen.

CHAPTER 11
LIFESTREAM – A RIVER

In the last chapter, I talked about life as a road. This time the metaphor is a river which I call the Lifestream. It is easy to imagine your life in linear terms, with a past, present, and future. You are born, you grow old, and finally you die. So it is not difficult to imagine your lifestream flowing out of the Godhead, which is the source of your life energy. When you are born, you come in with enormous life force energy, which you can call "endless possibility" which is available to you in whatever way you wish to use it. Everything is possible or attainable–until you start making choices.

Here's the perfect example: Infants make every single sound in the world when they begin gurgling and cooing. As they listen to the people talking around them, they mimic the sounds they hear in the intonation of the language they hear. If the parents are Chinese, they use tonality; if Xhosa, clicks. They choose those particular sounds so that when they do speak, they will make only those sounds from the language they hear, and eliminate the rest.

That is very similar to what happens emotionally. As you proceed down your lifestream, you make choices to break off or eliminate those parts of yourself that will hinder your receiving your allotted supply of love and sustenance. If, for example, you learn that yelling and screaming will cause you to be ignored or abused in some fashion, you may cut that angry/frustrated part of yourself off and become compliant–or you may find doing exactly the opposite gets you the attention you crave. None of these decisions are conscious, and they were made in the earliest stages of your life.

When you suppress one part of yourself, that causes your lifestream to split, creating a tributary that siphons away the part of you that is "boisterous and loud" or "soft and compliant". Even though you continue on with your life, you've become diminished to some degree. When you make the next decision to split off a part of yourself, you discard more pieces of yourself. Every

72

emotional decision that forces you to cut off parts of yours and diminishes you. The belief system that shackles your mind cuts oft more pieces of your lifestream. If you lose too much of your energy, you become prey to sickness.

As you can now imagine, at present, your lifestream is nowhere near as strong and powerful as when you were born. It's easy to realize how diminished your lifestream is because so much of it has been drained away by your life experiences.

Let's use shame as an example. Shame goes back to the earliest days of toddlerhood (before year one). Someone's (usually a parent's) ongoing disapproval or judgment about you provoked shame, which caused you to split off that unacceptable part of yourself. Continued disapproval created more shame branches, so that even more of your energy got diverted.

When you reclaim yourself and your energy, you begin to recognize how much energy you have lost.

Going Back

Since this book focuses on self-change, working on your lifestream can help you regain your energy by changing not only the past, but the future, as well. The Lifestream process does not change a *memory* (as we did in other chapters) but just reclaims the energy itself.

Your river looks like a root system—a multitude of thick or thin branches split off from a central stalk (see illustration, page 75). Each branch is a point where you lost some of your lifestream. If you were to dip your feet into the stream above any fork, you would sense what it felt like before you gave up that piece of energy. As you proceed farther back up the river, the quality of your lifestream energy feels far different from your energy today.

Lifestream work involves going back to those junctures where your energy branched off, healing the split, and directing all of those streams back into the main river so that energy will be available to you again.

It might sound really attractive to travel back to the original split and heal it, but it's like childhood healing work; you have to do it in stages. Otherwise the disruption to your psyche and your physical body can be devastating. Going back to that primordial branch for your first stab at lifestream work would cause an enormous upheaval inside you. You need to proceed slowly so all of your bodies can adjust to the changes.

Instead, choose a fairly recent time (last 20 years—not childhood) when you experienced a trauma, and block that streamlet. Doing so will give you more energy and more skill as you move back up the stream, healing earlier events.

You are likely to find, when you reach the branch, some kind of symbolic object sitting there, and it contains the energy that precipitated the split—which might from you or someone else. The object might look like stones, logs, statues, plugs—whatever your mind can conjure up. In all cases, the object *does not fit* the surroundings. You rarely find actual people at the forks, just their energy in some symbolic form, blocking your energy from you.

You must remove those objects—otherwise nothing can be done to reclaim the diverted stream. There are many ways to do that: You can pour gold acid onto them (harmless to you and your environment, but it melts the alien objects), invite the earth to swallow them up, or ask angels to remove them. Any of these methods releases the block from your space permanently.

Once the obstruction is removed, it becomes much easier to eliminate the fork itself. There are many images you can use. For this step, you can call on your Higher Self for help. Here are a few suggestions:
- Hire a bunch of beavers to create a dam.
- Use bulldozers to create a wide earthen dam.
- Dynamite the branch so it creates a landslide.
- Bring in some angels to create a magical barrier.
- Have the starship Enterprise blast in a dam using their phasers.
- Get creative.

Once you block off the split, that energy can no longer leach away from you. Not only do you remove the alien energy, you recover a piece of yourself that you lost, and you have altered your lifestream energy.

> *Gabrielle visualized herself taking a motorboat back to a branch that made her feel inadequate and helpless. There, she discovered a huge, howling stone statue of a close friend who had ridiculed her. Its sound cut right through her heart, so that she could barely think clearly. Her Higher Self stepped in and ordered the statue removed by angels. When that happened, she immediately felt a lightness in her heart.*
>
> *Then she called in beavers to construct a dam to block off that fork. Afterward, she recognized that this was the first step in healing her core issue of inadequacy fostered in childhood by her mother.*

After blockading a branch, when you sail back down the lifestream to the present, you may say to yourself, "Wait a minute. Why have I ended up at exactly the same point where I started? Nothing is different." Not true. Although your *outer* physical surroundings may look the same, you have shifted your *inner* emotional landscape because you have begun to reclaim your energy. It's like a dammed stream. The water left in the channel still runs down the streamlet bed but there is no more replenishing it.

Lifestream makes changes in your inner reality. This is what is so critical about this process. Regardless of what you may believe, that different inner reality that will eventually be reflected in your outer world sooner or later. You may not notice the difference today, next week, or next month, but sometime later you will discover that something that caused you shame no longer bothers you.

As you continue working backward, cutting off the streams, you regain your lifeforce energy and build up enough emotional strength to tackle earlier events. Eventually, you will have restored enough of your life force to reach the oldest events–whether you remember them or not.

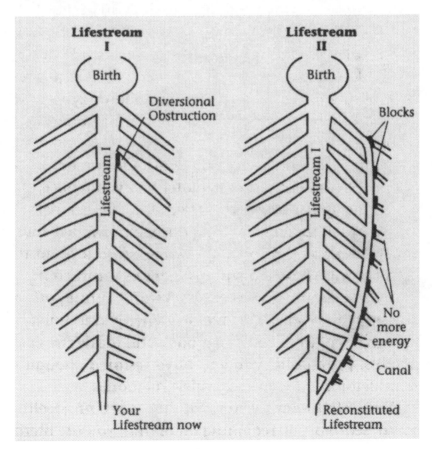

Your lifestream is your vitality, strength, feeling of power, of self-ness. By claiming all of that, you are literally creating a new person. You no longer can remain your "old self" with old feelings and responses, since there is no longer any internal support or energy for that old self to exist.

Changing Your Lifestream by Going Forward

If you don't want to make the long laborious journey back to earlier branches of your lifestream, you can do something different. You can change your lifestream by healing the river from *your present position*, creating a canal from one lifestream branch to another, so the life energy flows down into your river (see diagram, above).

This technique does not require you to go back and release memories. It just declares, "I've had enough of that behavior; I'm going to reclaim myself now." What you do is to use canals to create one river again.

It does not matter which technique you choose to use. You can work in both directions, since they both create powerful change. Repeat the exercise as often as you want.

EXERCISES

Going Back

1. Do your aura cleanout and bring yourself into present time.
2. Call in your Higher Self to assist you on this journey.
3. Summon a cloud, a helicopter, an enormous bird, boat, balloon, or any other conveyance to take you upstream.
4. Climb onto or into whatever shows up (both the bird and the cloud will be strong enough to hold you).
5. Instruct your Higher Self to guide your cloud/bird/helicopter/boat, etc., back to the particular branch you wish to work on. (If you don't know, your Higher Self does.)
6. Stop at the branch. It may get brighter, or you may feel a buzz or sign that says, "Here it is."
7. Look for the symbol that caused the split—a rock, ball, statue, sign, etc. Remove the object, with help from your Higher Self. Here are some examples:
   a. Call on angels to toss it into the sun.
   b. Call in a huge vat of gold liquid to pour over and dissolve the object.

    c.   Let the earth open up a fissure and suck the object down into it.

8. Call in helpers (beavers, bulldozers, workers, landslide, etc.) to create a strong high dam across the branch that cannot be breached.

9. Watch as the energy flows down into your lifestream.

10. Fly back downstream, and get off at your present time.

Going Forward

1. Do your aura cleanout and bring yourself into present time.

2. Call in your Higher Self to assist you on this journey.

3. Call in bulldozers, angels, or other assistants to create a canal between your river and the stream, so the water from the branch flows into your river.

4. Block off the branch beyond the canal so it cannot leach away any more water.

5. Watch the water flow into your river.

6. Put your feet in the river, and feel the new energy that has come back to you.

CHAPTER 12
CHANGING EMOTIONS

In Lifestream (Chapter 11), I described how to reclaim your energy in two ways—by going back to repair the original split, and also by creating canals to link the branches to the main stream in the present. In the same way we can change the emotional wiring in our brain without going back to change the past.

The emotional wiring in the limbic system of the brain (our emotional center) controls us, so that we act, think, and react in certain prescribed ways when faced with specific stimuli, unless we have spent a good amount of time working to break our patterns. When you go inside and change a childhood memory, you change those patterns and create new ones with different emotions. You can also call it "rewiring the brain".

The limbic system consists of many small bodies, some only a few cells in size, that produce massive effects in our emotional lives. Each of them has a specific purpose. Among them are the nucleus accumbens, the amygdala, the septum, and the locus coeruleus.

Here are some of the emotions ruled by these bodies: The amygdala deals with anger and aggression, so if you're feeling angry, your amygdala is being triggered. Your septum produces happiness. And the locus coeruleus seems to be directly connected with anxiety, and maybe even depression.

And then there is the nucleus accumbens; it is your pleasure center, where addicts get their high—whether it is from gambling or drugs or alcohol or sex, etc. Addicts feel an immense pleasure whenever they indulge—and to continue to get that "high", they'll do everything they can. Blame your nucleus accumbens for that.

That's one reason why it's so difficult for addicts to wean themselves off their drugs—who wants to give up feeling so good? Besides, the pleasure they feel when using prevents them from feeling the pain of their reality; their lives are often so bad that they would gladly obliterate the pain by addiction. (I'm simplifying a lot here; addiction has many components, but the pleasure stimulus is crucial in keeping someone addicted.)

Turning off the nucleus accumbens blocks you from getting that pleasure response from your addictive behavior. You may mourn the loss of the pleasure, but on the other hand, you can learn to enjoy other experiences that are not so self-destructive.

Metaphors

Our brains function in metaphors, the most obvious being language, which is an artificial construct your brain uses to interpret the world around us. Hence, most of what I have presented in this book has been metaphorical, so your brain can absorb it more easily.

Take this very simple and powerful sentence: "I'm tied in knots." You might actually visualize a KNOT. There are two interpretations you can make of that sentence (though it's a little more difficult because you are seeing the word on the page). If you speak the word, you might notice that there are actually two words that sound the same–KNOT and NOT. Context supposedly informs us of the "correct" meaning being expressed. You can see yourself being tied up in KNOTS, or you can sense the other metaphor of being tied in NOTS.

What does that mean, "tied up in NOTS"?

Specifically, it means stopped by things you cannot or will not or do not want to do/be/have. "I'm tied up in (k)nots" can mean *I'm all confused*, or *I have all these feelings of reluctance or Noes against doing something*. When you start exploring the KNOTS around a particular issue, you are sure to find the NOTS, the underlying emotional component.

"I'm all tied up in knots," Gregory said about whether he was going to take a job in another city at a much higher salary and level of responsibility. When we examined those knots together, he "discovered" all those NOTS that he "said" he wasn't aware of. Those NOTS included feelings of self-worth (how could he do the job?), of success (what if he failed?), of fear (what if he made the move and it was a disaster), and whether his family would support him–especially since his wife had a good job here. Those underlying NOTS were keeping him frozen and unable to make a decision. He had NOT been paying attention to what his brain was trying to tell him. (He ultimately turned down the job–too many NOTS.)

Metaphors are enormously powerful. The go into the subconscious mind and create change—so a positive metaphor will create positive movement, while a negative one (like those "nots") will cause stoppage or confusion. It's important to pay attention to the metaphors in your life—and how they control you. But for our purposes, I want you to see how metaphors can be used in a positive way to change your internal wiring.

The Lever

You are going to use the metaphor of the "lever" to change the wiring that is in your limbic system by adjusting a specific emotion up or down. You don't have to find a past event to heal the emotion you are working with. Just as with Lifestream, you can work with the structures themselves. Nor do you need to know which of the limbic bodies are being affected by your work—just the emotion you want to adjust. It is an effective way to disrupt the emotional hooks of the past by adjusting the present, and it serves as a powerful support for your healing work.

Imagine a panel with many vertical levers. These are the emotions. They are all stuck in the past, and are not in their optimum place. That means it is likely the levers of intense emotions such as anger or anxiety are stuck way up all the time, preventing your body from relaxing. That creates enormous and constant stress.

You need to adjust those levers down to their proper position—either UP or DOWN. Some emotions like anger, fear, depression, or anxiety belong at 1 or 2 most of the time.

When you need to call on a particular emotion—like anger—to deal with a present time situation, it's appropriate for the lever go up; but afterward, it should drop back down. That is the way healthy, functional emotion levers work. But that rarely happens.

The first step is to use the present time wand to bring these levers into present time. That clears a great deal of trapped energy. By making that adjustment, then, you are altering your inner patterns as you move all of yourself into the present.

You may still fall back on the old pattern, but it's no longer instinctive. You are also likely to feel somewhat uncomfortable because you have moved out of your comfort zone of predictability. That's how you are able to perceive that your wiring has been changed.

The emotions I am going to work on in this exercise are *anger* and *happiness*. Anger is usually fueled by the past. By adjusting the lever down, and continuing to push it down, it will cause emphatic changes to your brain. This does not mean you can't ever get angry; it just means that when you *do* get angry, the anger will be focused on the present situation–instead of triggering similar past situations, which immediately throws you out of present time.

Adjusting the Lever DOWN

1. Find a quiet spot. Clean out your aura and bring yourself into present time.
2. Call in your Higher Self.
3. With your eyes closed, imagine there is a panel in front of you with a number of vertical levers. All of these levers represent emotions that are regulated by the limbic system. You may see these levers, or sense them, or get nothing. Remember, just postulating that they are there is enough.
4. Take your present time wand and tap the panel several times. This panel is NOT in present time.
5. Put out your hand and grab the anger lever. You don't have to guess which one it is; your hand will find the right one.
6. Tap this lever with the present time wand three times.
7. Push the lever down. If you can only move the lever down one notch, that's all your body can handle. If possible, go down three notches. Three notches is a lot, but the more you can bring anger down, the better for your stress level.
8. Notice if there is any reaction in your body as you do that. A reaction means something in the past got triggered. Tap that body part with your present time wand because you need to stay in the here and now.
9. You will note a tab beside the lever. Its purpose is to lock the lever in place. Do that now. That prevents the lever from going back to its old position (old wiring that needs to be removed).
10. Ask your Higher Self to pour gold light onto the wiring being activated in your limbic system; that gold will dissolve the pattern of anger.

11. Every day or every few days, go back to this lever, and repeat steps 5-10.

Adjusting the Lever UP

If you want to make yourself feel good, put your hand on the happiness lever (not the pleasure lever). You can do this as part of the previous exercise, or do it separately. Just as the anger lever may drift back up, so the happiness lever is likely to go back down because you're not used to having happiness in your life. You need to keep nudging your happiness lever up.

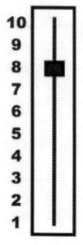

1. Repeat steps 1-4 above.
2. Put out your hand and grab the lever. You don't have to guess which one it is; your hand will find the right one.
3. Tap that lever with the present time wand and raise it three notches.
4. Repeat steps 8-11.

Chapter 13
Core Issues – The Soul

No matter how much work you do on yourself, do you keep stumbling over a basic issue that appears to color your entire life?

Congratulations! You have reached the core issue of your life. It permeates your entire being, and controls everything you think and do.

I have alluded on core beliefs in earlier chapters, but now it's time to put them into a larger perspective. I have found that there are three core issues or fears: fear of death, fear of abandonment, and fear of loss of self. They derive from some basic unfulfilled need–for safety, for love, or for being yourself.

A person who *fears death* defines life according to **survival**: "Will I be safe or will I be destroyed?"

A person who *fears abandonment* defines life according to **love**: "Will I get love, or be left with none?"

A person who *fears loss of Self* defines life according to **personal space**: "Will I have the right to be myself, or will someone intrude and take away my identity?"

The assessment you make about the world in the first twelve months of your life forms the foundation of your belief system. You then spend the next two years solidifying this belief. That means, if you spent your early months of life with an abusive family, but you were removed from that home and put into a loving, caring household, you probably had a very good chance of not developing a survival fear. If, however, the harmful situation persisted well into the first three years, it becomes very difficult for you to break that belief because the fear of death has become cemented into your cells.

These core fears may not appear obvious in your daily life, but they underlie your behavior, your feelings, your beliefs and thoughts, and control every one of your decisions and actions. Moreover, because of that unspoken fear, it is an easy step to accept anything that would provide you with safety, love, or self-identity.

The Three Core Beliefs

Fear of Death: When you have a core issue around survival, you judge everything according to *safety*. For you, survival is crucial. If you live in a war zone (whether it's in the inner city, a war-torn country, or a violent or rage-filled household), you are in terror for your life all the time. That fear of death creates a belief that you don't deserve to be alive, and, because of that, you don't deserve anything and must fight for everything you get. People with this belief are often filled with rage, that they either express or suppress, (except when they're drunk—and then the rage pours out) in order to stay alive.

All of your decisions, no matter how small, are life and death decisions. You prefer to function in black and white, rather than with shades of gray because that's safe and clear. Children see the world in absolutes, and so do adults livingwith the fear of death.

Normally, as you grow up, you learn to compromise and negotiate to get your needs met. You can function well enough—until you run into a threatening situation which throws you into survival mode. Then you react from your core fear. At a time like that, you don't worry about how much better it might be if you negotiated the issue. For you, it's all or nothing. Life or death. Those are your only alternatives.

There's a saying, "Half a loaf is better than none." Not if you're in survival mode. You can't have half a loaf because half a loaf means death. There is no half-life or half-death. It's all or nothing.

Fear of Abandonment: As a baby, if you did not get your emotional needs met, you will always crave what you are missing—enough love and attention to fill that hole left by neglect and abandonment (common examples are emotionally distant parents or parents who weren't attentive like drug using parents). When you feel abandoned, you believe you are unworthy of receiving love, which you learned was unattainable.

While the survivor clutches onto the loaf for dear life, you have no loaf at all, except for a few crumbs. In fact, you'd gladly do anything, even give away even those crumbs if it meant that someone would let you shower them with love (in the hope that they'd give you back some small modicum of attention).

That's why people who have an abandonment issue are usually codependents and caregivers; they'll endure all kinds of abuse in hope of gaining love, whether or not the other person had it to give in the first place. Unfortunately, abandoned people attract partners who are indifferent to their need for affection and prefer to keep them at arm's length because of their core issue, which tends to be loss of self.

Fear of Loss of Self: Imagine people grabbing at you, demanding that you pay attention to them, or intruding on your space, so that you feel overwhelmed, diminished and/or exhausted. In a situation like that, you believe you have no place that you can call your own—even your own Self. You always have the fear that you are going to be invaded—because you were.

As a baby you might have been fussed over constantly, and you found as you grew up that your boundaries were constantly being invaded. You were rarely allowed any privacy or time for yourself, nor did you feel that you were allowed by your caregivers to create your own identity.

Your body, your mind, even your soul are always under siege. (You need to do the exercises in Chapter 5–often.) Hence, you are afraid that you have no right to be your own person. (Those of you who are reading this book who feel abandonment will have a hard time understanding this core issue, which is diametrically opposite to yours. What you wouldn't do for such attention!)

Your reaction to the loaf is to clutch it protectively against your chest. "I won't give it to anyone!" you declare. Because of that, you may often be labeled as selfish, but it's because you're afraid of having parts of yourself taken away. Sharing the loaf without your agreement or permission equals invasion, so you set up strong, sometimes harsh boundaries to protect yourself.

Even with such high barriers, you still continue to worry that you're not strong enough to fend off emotional assaults on your identity. You are afraid a part of you will be snatched away. That's why you are very quick to defend your territory with "Do Not Trespass" signs. It's going to take a lot of trust-building before you create a doorway through your emotional walls, and you'll *never* want to bring them down.

Lack Of Love And Trust

These three core issues revolve around the lack of love and trust. You live with the assurance that your core fears will be activated again and again (being destroyed, abandoned, or smothered). If you aren't safe, you alternate between rage and acquiescence. If you feel abandoned, you reach out to anyone around for love. If you feel smothered and invaded, you create barriers for protection.

In *none* of these cases can you trust that you will get your needs met, so you're always hypervigilant, on the lookout for any situations or people that might trigger your core issue.

> *Xanthia was a codependent, always attuned to Colum, who complained that he was being smothered by her. She was underfoot, moaning over him, and begging for love. When she did that, Colum retreated. Xanthia was the abandoned Child begging for love, while Colum kept fighting for his space. The result was that the more he withdrew from her, the more frantically Xanthia threw herself at him. The situation worsened to the point that Colum never wanted to come home, which drove Xanthia into desperation and terror that he would leave.*

This example describes a very common and classic couple dynamic—of the giver and the taker—who exhibit the core issues of abandonment vs. loss of self. Healing this relationship meant finding ways for them to address and satisfy each other's core issue. In this couple's case, it meant creating time for them to do things together so Xanthia would feel loved, and specific structured time for Colum alone, so he wouldn't feel smothered. Shifting Xanthia's focus to other activities allowed her to stop fixating on Colum and his needs. After a while, Colum began to miss Xanthia's company and began paying more loving attention to her without her urging. She was thrilled to get what she had craved for so long—and without working at it.

> *For Goran, marriage had an all-or-nothing quality. If there was any kind of argument, he just knew that Charmaine would leave; so no matter what he really believed, he acquiesced to her and swallowed his anger. Finally, one day, he blew up during a minor disagreement; she was absolutely stunned by his shocking behavior, which seemed to come out of nowhere. When Goran told her that if he got mad, he thought she'd leave, Charmaine was shocked. Her response was "I thought you never cared enough about me to bother to give me your opinion—or show an emotion." To Goran, conflict was defined by his life/death issue, so he saw only one alternative, while she was looking to have a dialog.*

See how easy it is to interpret other people's motives according to our core issues? To help Goran feel safer, they set up rules for communication. They also learned each other's expectations for conflict. He began to realize that an argument didn't mean the end of the relationship (death); it just meant that there was a disagreement to be negotiated.

The True Depth Of Core Issues

When you trigger your core issue, your only motivation is to create safety for yourself in whatever way you function:

- When you are threatened by what you perceive as a life-threatening situation, you will automatically drop into a flight/fight mode.
- If you are feeling abandoned, you will be in terror over the loss of love.
- If you are feeling smothered, you will pull yourself behind a high wall.

Nothing can snap you out of that fear until you remove yourself from the situation–or the cause of the fear disappears.

Under normal conditions, calling in the nurturing love and joy from your Higher Self or angels can dilute that fear. However, when you are gripped by a core issue, it is almost impossible to feel anything positive and loving until you remove the stimulus.

If you believe that you are going to be destroyed, abandoned, or smothered, all the nurturing you get from your Higher Self and angels cannot penetrate through your haze of terror, until your adrenaline stops pumping, and you come back into reality; that's when you can see that the world is not as fearful as you imagined. Only then are you clear enough to accept comfort from your Higher Self and the angels.

Why is your core issue so potent and so intractable to normal processing? When you discover your particular core belief, you may sense a familiarity about it. That's because it does not exist simply in this lifetime. It has dominated most of your lives–and will continue to do so in future lifetimes until you resolve it.

Present life processing is like cleaning out one abscess after another, without addressing the whole symptom (like western medicine, which deals only with the symptoms, not the whole person). That's why simply working on it in your present lifetime doesn't break you free of its bonds. It is glued into your very soul. Only past life work really confronts the whole problem, letting you reach a point where you are cleaning out core issues at the very basic level of your being.

This terror is beyond your Inner Child. In fact, the huge waves of terror that are overwhelming her/him add intensity to your own fear. Having your Higher Self or an angel comfort the Child will take some of the pressure off you while you're spinning out of control.

The Soul

If you were to ask your Higher Self to take you back to the earliest occurrence of a core issue, you would find yourself in a past life and not just any past life—but a very early life. Core issue lifetimes are usually short—no more than three to five years long. Often you barely made it out of the womb. Just as the major issues of this life took time to settle in, so it was in the past.

After that, it took several lifetimes, one after another, to cement the core issue into your soul. These fears were then reinforced in later lifetimes until they became an integral part of your soul.

Every one of Lorena's relationships brought up her issues of abandonment. Her "lovers" demanded that she please them, and if she didn't, they'd leave. Finally, fed up with their abuse, and after much counseling, she decided to find the root of her crippling abandonment issue. During past life work, she went to one of the first lives after she decided to become a human being—very, very long ago. She saw a deformed newborn being abandoned by its mother, who projected tremendous disgust and revulsion at the baby's deformity. These emotions appeared as a viscid green slime that covered its body. Not only was the infant left to die, but having the abandonment overlaid with the mother's repulsion made Lorena feel utterly worthless and unloved.

Her first task was to clean the green slime off the baby. Then, with help from her Higher Self, she found a couple who delighted in the child, regardless of its deformity.

Shanda saw herself as a baby looking up at the blue sky. Suddenly a face with large sharp fangs came down over her head and ate her up. At that moment she felt shock and terror at her death. Her soul saw her mother, who had put the baby down on the grass, wail in horror and grief at losing her Child to the predator cat. Shanda, of course, sees the world as a dangerous place.

Such core issue life stories are not unusual.

Warning Signs

When you are caught up by a core issue, you probably will not realize what's going on with you. Here are some warning signs to tip you (and your friends) off:

- You simply cannot let something/someone go. It creates enormous emotional turmoil inside you.
- You feel completely ungrounded, unconnected to your Higher Self, Source, the angels, or to the earth. Nor can you ground yourself into reality, no matter what you do.
- You can't see your core issue clearly, nor do you have the ability to find any clarity. It's as if you're on a carousel spinning out of control. You have no balance or neutrality.

If you can recognize the times you are activated, then you can take steps to remove the fear-producing stimulus (for example, leaving the dangerous situation, finding a supportive, loving friend, retreating to a safe, private place), so you can reach an inner feeling of safety. Only then can you regain your adult equilibrium.

The Consequences Of Change

It's one thing to wrestle with the core issue in this lifetime; to go back and heal those early lifetimes means you are committed to changing something deeply profound inside of you–an essential piece of who you are, something that you have known, "loved", and "cherished" for most of your existence on earth. Your core issue has become part of the makeup of your soul. By chipping away at this blob, you are gradually changing into someone else–someone you don't know. That can be very intimidating. What kind of person are you likely to become?

When you work with the lifestream, it's not wise to go back upstream to the very first split in your river until you've united some of the branches closer to the present.

That won't cause a radical shift in your energy, which would be dangerously disruptive to all your bodies (one consequence is that you will get pretty sick). It takes time and effort to prepare yourself for such a dramatic energy shift.

Core issues are exactly the same. Tackle later lives first. When you've resolved those lifetimes, then you can handle the profound changes that will develop out of your core issue. Naturally, the earlier the lifetimes you work with, the stronger the payoff in this lifetime because you're going deeper and deeper into your soul. As you reconfigure those lives, you will find yourself having fewer inherent constraints on your beliefs, your attitudes, your behavior and your feeling toward yourself.

I cannot emphasize enough how critical core issue work is. It is profound, monumental, and daunting. Therefore, you may require the assistance of an expert to help you confront your issues, most particularly, a transpersonal psychotherapist who is receptive to working with past lives, present problems, and the Higher Self, angels and the Inner Child.

In addition, you can provide your own self support. One of the keys is to begin affirming that you are acceptable and okay (with the reassurance of your Higher Self and angels). Another key is to create situations that support self-acceptability, including participating in activities with acquaintances you enjoy, developing your own ability to create safety in your environment, and recognizing that your gifts are worthy of being shared with others. All this will help you reshape your attitudes about yourself and your core issue. As you do that work, it becomes much easier to let go of your old behaviors and beliefs. And continue to say affirmations.

What does a person who is free of their core issue look like? Happy. Relaxed. At peace. Loving. It's hard to know. Most of us aren't there. A clue to what it looks like is how you act when you are feeling comfortable, at ease, and in control and happy with yourself. The fear of abandonment, and self-loss sweeps over you less and less often. That means, you may still revert to that terror from core issue triggers, but the frequency and duration drop significantly as time passes. Under most circumstances, you can function as an adult, not a terrified child. To me that is a measure of progress–that you can keep the control of yourself more and more in your adult hands. That's a major step in healing.

Chapter 14
Past Lives

Up to now, you have been working on issues from your present life.

It's time to step back further into the past–into other lifetimes. You may have heard of reincarnation, and the idea that you have lived a number of different lifetimes, though you cannot remember them. Nevertheless, these lifetimes have an impact on the choices you have made and the life experiences you have, whether you are aware of them or not. In fact, once you start delving into the realm of past lives, behaviors that may seem confusing or incomprehensible in your life suddenly become much clearer, such as the reason for a particular illness or deformity or phobia or abuse.

John Donne said, "No man [or woman] is an island." Although he was talking about human relationships, it applies to our many lifetimes as well. We do not exist in a vacuum; our motivations, needs, and fears are connected to other lifetimes through our family, our associations, and our beliefs, through lessons learned, gifts given, persons encountered, and a hundred other reasons.

If you could relive your past lives, you would recognize similarities between them and your present life. There are similar (or identical) themes that carry over from lifetime to lifetime, recreating, yet again, those same experiences so you can resolve them; once that happens, they won't influence your next life.

Your parents, close friends, and significant others are usually intertwined with you, although it's not necessary that you recognize your mother from that lifetime as your child/parent/spouse/lover in this one. You all switch roles from lifetime to lifetime, like a repertory theater company.

Except for the fact that they take place in different times and milieus, and with different costumes, past life dramas have the same emotional entanglements. Good or bad things happen to you, your family, and others around you; and after a life filled with a variety of experiences, you die in some fashion. That, of course, is the key difference from this present life; there is a terminus–your death.

The following is a good example of a typical past life scenario.

Calleia always felt abandoned by her family, no matter how strongly they professed their love. One day I asked her to follow that feeling of abandonment back to its first occurrence. She found herself as a young child with her mother, trapped in a burning cottage. Although her mother desperately tried to get them out, she was overcome by the smoke. With tears streaming down her face, Calleia watched this scenario unfold. She realized that her mother had really been trying to save her that from the flames, though unsuccessfully, leaving the terrified child to perish abandoned and helpless.

Healing your childhood issues helps a great deal; but past life work heals both that life, as well as *this* one (two good deeds for the price of one). When you resolve your issue in a past life, you no longer need to revisit that same issue, lifetime after lifetime. Its effects in your present life will diminish.

How can you tell when you are dealing with a past life issue? Very simple. No matter how much you work on your problem, it never quite seems to get resolved. While present life work nibbles at its edges, you can never get to its heart–until you go into a past life. Your past lives contain traumas in the form of karmic debts, uncompleted agreements, and unfulfilled tasks that your soul would be more than grateful to put paid to.

It may take a number of lifetimes to unsnarl the emotional knots because there is so much "juice" (unfinished business) among all of you, which cannot reasonably get resolved in one lifetime, and indeed, may be increased in the current life. Changing past lives can provide as much benefit as resolving your present life issues. By handling the situation back then, though, the issue will stop accumulating more energy in this life–or the next. The result not only changes your life now, sometimes dramatically, but it also heals the other people involved in the events, as well.

Multiple Lives

Suppose that, instead of happening one after another, those "past lives" all exist simultaneously even though they "appear" to take place over thousands of years.

This idea of "simultaneous" lives was first described in the book *The Education Of Oversoul Seven* by Jane Roberts. In this theory, linear time is only a construct, not a reality (with which Einstein would agree). I find it very apt in this work because you can see the impact of the changes more easily.

Imagine a spoked wheel with a hub in the center. The hub is where your Oversoul lives, overseeing all the lifetimes, past, present, and future, and the spokes are your lifetimes. When a particular life (spoke) gets activated (for example, by meeting someone who was important to you in another lifetime), it comes down into the hub to be worked on. Any changes made to that lifetime then flow down all the spokes and alter the other lives accordingly. Although you only see its effects from the perspective of here and now, if you had the opportunity to sit in the Oversoul's seat at the center of the hub, you could see the results radiate across the vast tapestry of your many lifetimes.

That means if you atone for being a miser in a past life, your relationship with money in other lives shifts. Or if you dissolve a sticky love agreement, that frees you both in all those lives where you two were lovers. This ripple effect spreads throughout all of your collected life experience (including future lives on this planet), lives on other planets, and parallel lives.

Reactions

Just the *idea* of past life work may provoke a strong reaction in you—particularly from your mind's loud objections to the idea, and then to whatever you see or sense. When you find a past life, especially if you believe there's no such thing—such an assault on your belief system can be shocking—particularly, if the experience is very vivid and intense. Expect your mind to argue vociferously against the validity of what you saw. Just remember not to succumb to its arguments and invalidate your experience. What's important is the *result*, whatever your belief.

You may feel upset, angry, or embarrassed because what you see is unacceptable, unpleasant, or just plain crazy. That's your mind and your belief system getting in the way again.

> *When Aisha went to the first occurrence of her issue, she found herself on an asteroid trying to escape from aliens (she did believe in reincarnation, but not extraterrestrials). Even with her judgment about what she was seeing, she had a monumentally profound experience that completely changed her life.*

Finally, you may blame your past life persona for the terrible deeds he/she committed, or get angry at how foolish your persona acted (of course you'd never do such a stupid thing!), and want them to suffer—except that you're the one who's suffering now.

You may experience any or all of those feelings before, during, and after the journey. They still won't affect what goes on during the experience, as long as you are willing to continue the process. You just need to hang in there—and keep breathing. Remember, your Higher Self brought you to this event to help your healing.

Karma

A simple explanation of karma is a kind of cosmic balance sheet, listing your personal accounts payable (bad deeds) and accounts receivable (good deeds). No collection agency comes after you to hound you for those back debts, nor does God force you to pay by causing you to burn in hell. It's your responsibility alone, and your Higher Self handles the repayment by finding some way for you to balance your debt. Very simply, that means if you hurt someone in one life, he or she gets to reciprocate in another.

After you die, your Higher Self assesses your life, dispassionately but lovingly, and tallies up those karmic debts. If your good deeds outweighed the bad, you may get to cancel some of your accounts payable. For the debts that were not resolved or canceled, the Oversoul then decides what kinds of lessons in another lifetime will give you an opportunity to complete the payback.

It may take many lifetimes for you to get up the nerve (or strength) to pay a particular debt (knowing that it will cause you pain, for you will have to put yourself into a situation where what you did to others gets done to you (sounds like the Golden Rule, doesn't it?). That's why people who rape and torture get abused and crippled by their erstwhile victims in another life.

> *Aliena had a very bad marriage. Although she loved and supported her husband emotionally and financially, he had affairs and abused her emotionally all the time. In the past life that had precipitated this karmic payback, she was a wastrel and opportunist who seduced and married a rich, homely woman, beat and mistreated her, whored around, squandered her fortune, and ultimately drove her to suicide. Her present life husband was that woman, who was exacting her (his) retribution by doing the same thing to Aliena now. Seeing that lifetime made Aliena very sad, and yet she was also relieved to know the reason for her misery.*

It's easier to deal with lifetimes in which you were the victim, not the villain. Unfortunately, we all have a number of bad lifetimes, along with one or two evil ones. (*Bad* means something like raping and pillaging–and usually involves you and few other people; it also has always been a generally acceptable, if unpleasant, reality throughout history. *Evil* is Stalin, Hitler, the Nazis and other genocidal maniacs, who actively pursued torture and genocide–there is a vast karmic difference between *bad* and *evil*.) In past life work, you get to see yourself exhibit all kinds of unpleasant behaviors–mostly in the *bad* category.

> *Branwyn couldn't get past the belief that she "owed" her parents the right to hurt and abuse her–which they did, both physically and emotionally, all through her childhood. That statement smacked of karmic debt. When we followed her feeling back to its source, she saw a time when her parents were her slaves, whom she badly mistreated.*

Having your rotten lives exposed can bring up shame over your less-than-stellar performance. Since you have severe judgments over your present day "faults," however large or small they might be, you may feel the impact even more when you find out about your bad deeds in your previous life.

As you wallow in your guilt when you see such a life, you need to remember that you're watching an *entirely different lifetime*! You are NOT that jerk/creep/lowlife/scum. If you are reading this book, you are a decent person trying to understand how to heal and evolve. You can anguish over those past mistakes, but don't dwell on them. Simply work on your karma.

What signals a "karmic debt?"

- The same issues come up over and over again with no measurable release.
- You keep talking about owing, or guilt or obligation, or you have an almost obsessive need for taking care of someone, even if it isn't overtly expressed (severe codependency and addiction may be part of this dynamic. Addicts often don't want to face the responsibility and concomitant pain of their karmic obligation, so it just adds to their debt).
- You have lots of intensity around the issue, far outweighing its importance.

When you've cleared the karmic debt, you will notice the following changes:

- A significant drop in your intensity around it;
- A gigantic drop in your obsessive need to owe or pay back and a willingness to break free of old codependent or addictive patterns.
- An almost inexplicable but tangible feeling of relief, spreading throughout your body and soul.

Agreements

Agreements are dyad links forged between you and another person, usually for some purpose, and often for a particular length of time. They include teacher/student, business associates, helpers, lovers–in other words, all the normal interpersonal connections you create in your life. They help you form bonds of support and caring that give your life meaning. Agreements maybe short-lived (days, weeks, months), or extend for years or decades.

The problem arises when the agreements you made unwittingly remain in force across lifetimes. They contain words like "always" and "never" and "forever" (as in "I'll love you forever," or "We'll never let each other go"). "Forever" doesn't mean until you die, but for *ever*–lifetime after lifetime after lifetime.

Such unreleased agreements impede your growth and development by welding you two together, regardless of your present circumstances and development. That means what was once a viable relationship can turn into a crippling twisted burden, until you break the bond (or go nuts trying).

Many a person has found, when trying to shed a destructive relationship, that a "forever" chain binds the two parties together, trapping both of their energies in that long-forgotten agreement. No matter how much work you do on yourself, nothing can really shift until your agreement is dissolved.

> *Temperance was incapable of breaking up from a neglectful lover. She suffered endless heartache, while he played around, yet could not give him up, even after extensive therapy to work on her dependency issues. In a past life, she heard herself swear to love this man forever, just before he went off to war and never came back. So here she was, holding on to that oath, lifetimes beyond its usefulness, and she was desperate to be free of it. Once she dissolved that agreement, it was amazingly easy for her to shed her boyfriend and get on with her life—much to the relief of everyone around her.*

Breaking an agreement is easy. You don't need a past life journey, just a decision by one of the participants to let go.

Some people become afraid that without an agreement, there will be nothing to hold the relationship together. If, when you dissolve the agreement, the relationship ends, it was not healthy or viable anyway, and was long overdue for termination. Any reason for staying together was long gone. Moreover, you want something that is healthy and supportive of who you are—not who you were lifetimes ago!

Divine Help

When delving into your past lives, it is important to have at least one ally who is loving, caring, and strong, who sees you clearly and with complete love and acceptance, who can protect you from some of the personal "demons" who inhabit your past. That ally can be your Higher Self, or angels. Because they are in contact with all of your many lives, any of them can take you directly to the situation that resonates with this lifetime's issues.

Chapter 15
Changing A Past Life

Even though your mind (and friends/relatives) may try to convince you otherwise, you *can* reach a past life. It simply takes willingness on your part. Right now, you may want only to find out what happened during one of your lifetimes—after all, it takes time to adjust to the idea of past lives (although I've found that many people who *say* they doubt the concept are intensely curious about their own past lives). If you are willing to change the story as you did with your childhood memories, you can apply your modern perceptions, your Higher Self's innate wisdom and/or angelic love, toward creating a new, positive result in that life—and in this one.

The most effective route to a past life is identical to present life work—following a body sensation back to an event—but this time you want to go back to the *first* occurrence of the trauma—which usually ends up somewhere far different from childhood.

Calleia, who wanted to go to the origin of her abandonment issues, ended up dying in a burning cottage (which was completely outside her expectation—or beliefs).

If you worry about finding a past life, I suggest a mild self-hypnotic induction that you can practice. It helps to create a recording that you can listen to as you get ready for your inner journey: Call on your Higher Self, and, with your hand in hers, *slowly* go down a staircase, step by step. At the bottom you will find a door that, when you open it, will take you to the first occurrence of your particular issue. The door represents a clear demarcation of realities, moving from an outer, logical world into your inner, magical, non-logical unconscious where all things are possible.

Once you and your Higher Self reach the scene, take a few moments to tune into the situation. Do not *imagine* what you *ought* to see or create an expected scenario. Just accept whatever comes up to be there. Your mind will try, as usual, to get in the way with its comments, especially if you have some knowledge of a particular time period. Just thank it and focus on your inner movie.

What's happening? Who are the major characters or personae? Who is doing what to whom? You may get images or simply feelings. I'm continually surprised by what people come up with, and the stories are rarely what they (or I) expect.

Trust that your Higher Self knows that what it's showing you is right. It may mean watching your own death. That's why your Higher Self needs to accompany you on these journeys, to remind you that you are never alone or resourceless or helpless, so you can observe what happens with some neutrality: "I see my character being killed by brigands." "I'm raping and pillaging that poor defenseless village." And so on.

You will have a chance to reprogram your life once you have seen what happened.

Occasionally, you may find yourself merging with your past life persona, just as you merged with your Inner Child, so that you are actually in the scene. I don't encourage that. It's better to remain a separate, invisible observer. There are two reasons for this.

1) If the event is traumatic, just as with your childhood, you can get overwhelmed by the drama; and

2) If you stay merged with your persona, you begin to see with that persona's world view. Changing a past life situation requires your *modern* perspective–so remain separate.

To unmerge yourself from your persona, have your Higher Self take your hand and pull you out of your persona.

Making Changes

There are two kinds of past life changes you would normally make: 1) saving someone (usually yourself) from harm, and 2) resolving/healing karmic issues. Either one involves some level of intervention.

My rule of thumb for all my work (in past and present lifetimes) is **go for safety**. Make your persona *safe* before doing anything else. Surprisingly, just doing that can cause an enormous shift (since that often means saving them from unpleasant death).

Nyla consistently got trapped in dangerous situations (both emotional and physical) in this lifetime. In a past life, she saw her persona stoned to death by her neighbors who feared her because she was "different" (a relative newcomer to their village). She realized that her persona had to leave that place to survive. To reconfigure that lifetime, Nyla guided her persona to the river where a boat was waiting to take her to safety—to another more-welcoming village. She then watched her persona marry, raise a family, and die, having then experienced a totally different life from the trapped, traumatic lifetime she actually "lived".

Calleia (of the burning cottage) wanted to save her mother and herself. Her Higher Self suggested, "Turn around and look for the door. " The next thing I heard was, "We're safe!" When she came back from her journey, Calleia said, "I'm amazed at what happened. As soon as I saw that door, my mother grabbed me and tore out of there." She added, "I understand now that my mother loved me. She didn't abandon me intentionally." That was what she needed to break the hold of her abandonment issue. She still had present life issues to resolve, but the root cause had been removed.

One of the key factors in past life work is the ability to blend into the situation in order to take control of the action. If you appear as your modern self to a person living in the Middle Ages, she'd be convinced you were the devil leading her into hell. That's because her worldview allows for only two kinds of supernatural beings—angels and devils, and since most strangers are devils, that's what you must be. To get around that, you must use the metaphor of the time period—in other words, present yourself as an emissary of God, i.e., an angel. To someone in ancient times, you would be a goddess, god, or nature spirit.

In the inner world, you are allowed to make all kinds of suggestions to further or change the action, for they are accepted as totally normal, as long as they are *consistent with the scenario*. Anachronisms definitely cause concern. In other words, no airplanes, telephones, or computers in prehistoric times.

In a lifetime in Atlantis, Felicia heard and saw a telephone ringing. After some discussion with me about it, she decided that since Atlantis was a technologically advanced civilization, maybe they did have telephones. Only after coming to that conclusion could she continue with her process.

If you want to change the scenario, you need to do it wisely, so that the results will be both satisfactory for that time—and for you here and now. Some kinds of change are simple. When I've made a suggestion like, "Find the door and leave now," I've rarely had a client say, "There's no such thing." Rather they see it, open it, and walk right through, like Calleia did.

And then there is your mind. It is desperately striving to make logical sense of what is going on (as best it can under the circumstances). It will question the legitimacy of any suggestions, never mind being in a past life! To calm it down, I say something like, "In the inner world everything is possible." That sentence does a lot to sooth its outrage.

You will not go wrong by asking your Higher Self or an angel, "What do I do next?" Your Higher Self will give you very clear and simple answers like, "Find the door," or "Take the boat". Pass those instructions on to your persona. It's rare that your persona will argue with your suggestion. If he or she does, remind them that whatever they've done so for hasn't worked very well. If necessary, take the persona's hand and guide him or her to wherever you want them to go, as Nyla did.

> *Damaris always wanted to be top dog in every kind of relationship with men. In going to the source of her fierce need for control, she saw herself as a priestess of the goddess at the time when the warriors of the patriarchal religion conquered her village, including the chieftain's ritually raping her. Unable to fight him off physically, she shut him off emotionally. She vowed she would **never** again be put in such a powerless position by a man (i.e., **forever!**).*
>
> *After viewing the situation, she and her Higher Self formulated a different outcome. Since both the priestess and warrior recognized that change was inevitable, and neither liked the obvious solution, Damaris, in goddess form, suggested an alternative—that the priestess and the warrior treat each other with respect instead of brutality and contempt, and turn the "rape" into a "joining of forces." Not only did both parties gratefully accept this solution (the priestess was attracted to the barbarian chieftain), Damaris experienced a marked shift in her own attitude toward men.*

After you've resolved your persona's situation, sit back and watch the new life unfold as if viewing a movie. This last step is eminently satisfying, to see how their life improved after you rescued them from disaster. It's like you're watching a movie. You don't have to do any work.

Karmic Payback

It's easy to create a new outcome that saves your persona from some dire fate for a life in which you were the victim. However, if your persona was the *perpetrator* of misery to others, you're going to feel other kinds of emotion (like shame, guilt, and horror) for what that persona did. Making the required atonement is going to be hard because you're going to have a difficult time remaining neutral or non-judgmental.

Karmic work creates the most intense resolution because it exposes you to your most unpleasant selves. Conversely, the payoff for completing it is the highest. Releasing karma not only frees up enormous energy, but it creates great big chunks of healing in your soul, as well as in your life.

Luckily, you don't have to do this healing work alone. You have angels and your Higher Self to handle any rectification—and you know they will be decent, caring, and dispassionate.

> *Martita was a spiritual junkie; she took every metaphysical workshop and class, desperately trying to unlock her psychic powers. While all her friends were having psychic visions, doing channeling, seeing auras—nothing seemed to work for her. When we searched for the cause of her inability to open psychically, she learned that she was under a karmic "injunction"; in other lifetimes, she had used her very powerful psychic powers for evil purposes. Her punishment now was to have them locked away when she really wanted to use them for good. This caused her enormous anguish; yet she recognized it was a fitting karmic atonement.*

Watching a lifetime like that will be painful, but you can hit the Pause button, and revisit it later on when you feel strong enough to continue. There's no deadline or timetable for doing such work. Just tell your Higher Self that you want to stop working on that past life for now. And don't forget to keep breathing deeply. It helps release your energy and your feelings and judgments.

If you feel capable of resolving the karmic payback, treat the incident as though you were dealing with childhood abuse. When you ask, "What needs to be done to this abuser so that he atones for his deeds?" your Higher Self will provide the appropriate answer, as usual.

The abuser must be punished. It helps a lot if he/she pays as much karmic debt as possible, then and there, in that lifetime. Often the persona will acknowledge his or her wickedness , and accept atonement–but don't be surprised if sometimes they refuse to acknowledge their bad deeds. When that happens, it means *you're* stuck with "suffering" the consequences in this *present* life. Yet that doesn't have to be the final answer. Angels can forgive certain amounts of karmic debt, if they deem it appropriate. You can ask them to determine when you have paid enough.

When you have completed your karma, it's very easy to recognize and experience it. It feels like a vast wave of relief, gratitude, and sadness sweeping through you, taking away pain–and leaving you light and joyous (until the next issue arises).

So...Is Any of This Real?

After any past life experience is over, you may have one big question: Was it real? Your logical mind may argue that changing the past life doesn't make rational sense (if it wasn't just your imagination).

It doesn't matter.

What is important is not the *label* you place on the experience, but the *experience* itself. You can't go back to that lifetime except in your mind (those folks are long since dead and buried). Instead, consider this: Did you experience some kind of change or transformation? Did you emerge with a different understanding or feeling?

Those are the criteria for measuring meaningful change. By providing whatever support your persona needs to choose a different option for his or her life, the experience ceased to be a traumatic soul wound. In almost every case where clients healed a past life, their present life underwent some kind of tangible shift.

By healing a past life trauma, you free up centuries of trapped energy for your use now. You get to see and feel the result in that life–and inside you now. Moreover, the benefits of past life work go far beyond just you.

When you untangle a past life knot, the other people involved in that past life scenario get healing too, whether they know it or not. Although the results may not be obvious, at least at first, they will become apparent as the months go by. When you heal an emotional entanglement you can proceed to create other healthier connections with those persons if you choose, or disconnect from them permanently without hostility, anger or more karmic debt.

EXERCISES

Healing A Past Life

1. Call in your Higher Self or guardian angel. Ask them to take you down a flight of stairs to the appropriate lifetime. (You may want to prerecord this induction or use the one on my website., arianasarris.com)

2. Hand in hand, go down the stairs. Say, "I am going back to the first occurrence of [fill in your issue]." With each step down, you move back years or centuries to the first occurrence of your issue.

3. At the bottom is the door that will open directly to the lifetime you are looking for. Step through into that lifetime.

4. Be the unseen observer in the scene. If you aren't seeing or feeling anything, ask that your Higher Self describe the critical event. Don't let your mind make things up! Just relax and get a sense of the scene.

5. If you have merged with the persona, ask your Higher Self pull you out of the persona's body. You need to watch this story with modern eyes.

6. Watch what happens. That may mean seeing your persona's death.

7. Just doing these steps may be enough for you at this time. If so, go back through the door, back up the stairs, and open your eyes.

If you wish to release the trauma, follow the next few steps.

1. Rewind the past life "recording" to a time before the crucial event (like your death).

2. Find a way to help your persona resolve the painful or deadly situation. Ask your Higher Self what to do. It knows exactly what you need.

3. Follow its advice. That may mean becoming visible in a way that fits the society to give advice to the persona ("find the door, "follow the path").

4. Show or give the persona appropriate props, like a boat, a door, a tool, to further guide him to safety or resolution.

5. If your persona is the villain, ask your Higher Self to handle any punishment required to resolve the situation. You don't

have to get involved in the process, merely remain an observer of the scenario.

6. Observe the newly reconstructed life until the persona's death. Doing so gives that life and your soul a sense of completion.

7. Thank your Higher Self, and come back up the stairs.

If you are concerned about doing the process "right", have a friend read these instructions to you while you go through your journey, or record it and follow the steps. By the way, I have found that clients will stop in the middle of the process and discuss something with me (like Felicia with the telephones in Atlantis). You'll be amazed at how easy it is to go right back into your scenario and continue your work.

Breaking An Agreement

Agreements involve concepts like "forever" and "always" that last through many lifetimes. These need to be dissolved. If you still want to have a relationship with the person in this lifetime, you can make an agreement that continues until the end of *this* life.

1. Close your eyes. Take yourself into a room inside your head which holds a lot of files. Be sure there is a fireplace burning.

2. Ask that your Higher Self join you and bring the agreement you want to break. Visualize it as a piece of paper or scroll with writing.

3. Write "Canceled" or "Void" on your agreement (actually write the word in the air) with a red magic marker.

4. Tear it up and burn the pieces in the fireplace.

5. Say, "I release you" three times.

And that's the end of your agreement with that person.

Chapter 16
Phobias – The Aura

What is it you fear most? Is there a reason for your "fear? Or is it inexplicable, seemingly irrational, at least to others?

Some of us harbor unreasonable fears of spiders or snakes, or cats, or sleep, or the number 13, or high or small places, or that we'll be squashed to death, or a hundred and one other terrors. There is no logical reason for these terrors, so they are labeled as *phobias*.

The dictionary describes a phobia as a "persistent, irrational, abnormal or intense fear of something without any obvious cause" (the word means "fear" in Greek). Your brain is wired in such a way that the stimulus completely bypasses your logical mind and goes straight into the reptilian brain, triggering a wildly extreme physical reaction. Your heart races and pounds, and your legs turn to jelly; you are beyond reason. Terror courses through you; and all you want to do is flee.

Some of us can cope with our fears in our everyday lives, while others are incapacitated by their phobias. When you are in the grip of a phobia, you cannot think clearly. Familiar and common phobias include agoraphobia (fear of open spaces and crowds), acrophobia (fear of heights), claustrophobia (fear of small enclosed places), and arachnophobia (fear of spiders).

People who experience an earthquake or survive the unrelenting horror of war, or develop claustrophobia from a situational trigger, such as being shut in a closet when they were small, suffer from post-traumatic stress, a strong emotional reaction to that event that may be resolved over time with specific psychotherapeutic techniques (like Emotional Field Therapy). Phobias, on the other hand, with their intensely strong body reactions, don't seem to have any obvious cause. The fear has always been with you.

I am acrophobic (afraid of heights), but nothing in my past explains why I suffer from it. How did I get it? No one in my family knows. I rarely find my phobia a problem simply because I tend to avoid heights. When I happen to look down from a high place, I get a rush of terror, my legs turn to gelatin, and I can clearly envision myself falling off the building, and landing at the bottom in a bloody mush.

Sometimes when I feel brave, I attempt to confront my terror. It once took me about a half hour to climb up 140 steps to an ancient kiva in Bandelier National Park. It was very hard to find some rationality or calmness through my terror, but I just kept breathing deeply to calm myself, while a friend massaged my shoulders to help me relax. Eventually, I made it to the top, but I fought for every single step I took.

Talk therapy is woefully unsuccessful, as Freud himself found out. The only recognized "successful" treatment is behavioral modification through gradual sensory desensitization (which is its only goal), not resolving the issue.

It works like this: if you are afraid of bridges, you first learn to relax (using deep breathing and meditation techniques). Then you are shown a picture of a bridge (the stimulus). As your normal terror reaction kicks in, you use your relaxation techniques to calm down. When the terror becomes too intolerable, you remove the picture and relax. Gradually, you increase your tolerance of the bridge picture. Then the stakes are upped. You drive by a bridge, and when you can handle that, you stop at the bridge, and so on. You overcome the debilitating effects of the terror so you can function without being overwhelmed. However, the phobia is still there—underneath. All you did was get desensitized to it—but for many people, that is enough.

The origin of the terror can never be addressed or removed because phobias have no triggering mechanism in this lifetime; they come from some past life experience. Standard past life work focuses on repairing incomplete issues or repaying karmic debts that relate to your present life situation. That unfinished business creates similar circumstances in your many lifetimes until the issue gets resolved, but does not provoke the soul-searing terror that a phobia triggers.

Somehow in a past lifetime, you had an experience that traumatized your *soul*. Usually, it had to do with a violent form of your death. Now your soul reacts in terror when the situation is re-created in some way (like a claustrophobe getting into an elevator). Because of having that violent experience of death, your life's work may not have been completed; and you have a death trauma that remains unresolved.

> *Hallam had an irrational fear of enclosed areas; and every time he stepped into an elevator or closet, he felt a rush of panic so strong that he was afraid he'd start choking to death. This panic persisted, even after years of psychotherapy in a fruitless search for its cause. Behavior modification relieved the symptoms. Eventually, wanting to get to the root of the phobia, he decided to do past life work. Almost immediately, he found himself trapped in a cave that had collapsed, crushing his chest so he could not breathe. He died of asphyxiation. As soon as Hallam saw that, he reshaped the memory by getting someone to rescue him, so he could survive. As a result the claustrophobia vanished.*

Etheric Energy

Parapsychologists and psychics who investigate haunted houses often find that the ghosts who inhabit such dwellings were killed violently, or suffered a fatal accident so abruptly and unexpectedly that they did not really realize that they had died. They were in a kind of shock; while their essence (soul) moved on, their etheric body (aura) remained stuck in that location on the physical earth plane, still believing that they were alive. When the psychics helped the ghosts recognize that their body was dead, the auras no longer had any connection to that place and could then dissipate; and most did so.

What that means is, if you suffer a violent death, your soul departs your dead body without bringing away all of your essence. Because a fragment of your etheric body gets stuck in that one place, you lose that piece of energy from your soul. That means your soul is incomplete.

If you don't reclaim that lost etheric energy in the next lifetime (and you probably won't because you don't know that something is missing), the trauma remains embedded, lifetime after lifetime, so that whenever a resonating or similar situation arises, the soul immediately reacts. This is what creates the phobia.

Not only was your soul traumatized by your energy loss, it was also traumatized by the violent experience that caused it. That's another mark of a phobia—an enormous rush of adrenaline that floods the body and soul, searing the soul at that moment with incredible fear.

When your soul takes possession of a new body, it immediately imprints that body with its terror and loss. Over many lifetimes the soul's loss gets stamped on each physical body as an intense irrational fear. The phobia is not something your mental and emotional bodies can understand or deal with. It is mysterious and irrational.

Clearing Phobias

Clearing a phobia requires going back to the affected past life, using the intensity of the terror as the hook, and resolving the original experience. Once you access the original phobia experience, you can proceed with the normal past life healing, transforming the event by providing an alternative reality for your persona. When you do so, the piece of the soul that was missing can finally be retrieved, and in so doing, allow the imprinted trauma to be released from the soul's field.

Resolving a phobia is a soul/aura healing. That kind of work causes powerful alterations in your brain patterns, just like altering childhood traumas impacts your Inner Child. The neuron pathways to that event get disconnected so that your body doesn't react in the same way. Because the physical body bears the brunt of the trauma, every time the stimulus gets triggered, you may feel some physical twinges, but nothing like the full assault of terror, as before.

When Hallam created a different outcome for his life story, not only did he resolve his death, but he healed the soul trauma by retrieving that missing piece of himself after many lifetimes.

Jerome had such a fear of heights that he couldn't even approach a second-story window. In regression, he went back to a lifetime when he ws the designated human sacrifice. He was incredibly terrified when the villagers dragged him up to the cliff, catatonic with fear as they tossed him off the cliff, and in total terror as he hurtled onto the rocks below, where his smashed and broken body suffered a quick but painful death. All of that enormous terror marked his soul.

To change that life, his Higher Self talked with the local god, who then explained to the villagers that human sacrifice without a willing victim was worthless, so they needed to find someone who would die willingly. The villagers immediately set Jerome free. Interestingly enough, in his newly reconstructed life, Jerome came back to the village in his old age and offered to be the willing sacrifice. Although he still died the same way, this time his attitude was markedly different. His leap over the cliff was tranquil and joyous, no longer a trauma but an epiphany. By choosing that death at his time, not theirs, it resolved his acrophobia.

EXERCISE

Healing A Phobia

When you resolve a phobia, you can follow most of the steps for past life work (see Chapter 13).

1. Go back to the past life.
2. Bring in the Higher Self who will be *really* glad to help you resolve the lifetime.
3. Change the experience so it doesn't end with the same tragedy.
4. Follow the lifetime through, and watch your character die.
5. Bring yourself to your inner sanctuary.
6. Call back your lost energy. Say something like, "I call all my energy back from that phobia-creating lifetime." Imagine it flowing into your body. Mechanisms may include any of the following (or whatever works for you).

    • Become a magnet that attracts your energy to you.
    • Let your Higher Self sit in the middle of your sanctuary and breathe in the returning energy.
    • Let the energy become heavy and fall to the ground. Gather it up and pour it into yourself through the top of your head.
    • Turn it into a cloak and wrap it around you.
    • Pick your own image.

CHAPTER 17
HEALING DISEASE

My friend Marlene's diabetes caused the bones in her right foot to collapse, but with an orthopedic shoe she could walk on the foot without serious pain. Imagine my surprise when I learned she was in the hospital, where her doctors insisted that her foot be amputated because it was rotting and gangrenous. She was frantically resisting their pressure, and looking for a more wholistic alternative.

Before anything could be done with her foot, we needed to find the cause of her foot problem and heal it non-surgically. I suggested that she ask her Higher Self to transport her back to the time when the body made the decision to lose the foot. She saw a lifetime when she was a trapper who had gotten his foot caught in a bear trap: the trap's teeth had clamped down exactly on the spot where her present-life arch had disintegrated. Although the trapper managed to free himself from the bear trap with extreme difficulty, he lost the foot in the process. The resulting wound became gangrenous, and he died.

In order for that imprinting to be removed from her own foot, Marlene needed to transform that past life. Taking on the form of a spirit, she sought out help for the trapper and found a large, strong man to rescue him. The stranger not only opened the trap, but he took the trapper to his hut to dress the wound.

Although the foot bones were crunched, they did not become infected, and the trapper recovered, with a limp–Marlene has a slight one now–and no loss of foot or life.

After she recreated the lifetime, I asked Marlene what her foot needed to heal. She got the image of cherry bark being wrapped around the arch, across the broken bones. She envisioned herself doing that, both in the prior lifetime, and in this one. Within four days, the suppurating abscess had disappeared, and her skin was fresh and healthy. Her amazed doctors agreed that an operation was now unnecessary and sent her home.

By releasing the body's wounding in her past life, that long-ago trauma became a memory, and the resonance that recreated the experience in this life was disrupted, obviating the loss of the foot in this present body.

Symptoms

Where does your body hurt? Common "hot spots," in your body include the stomach, chest, back, neck and shoulders, and head—each with its associated ailments, such as backaches, neckaches, and headaches; colds (chest or head); ulcers or other gastric or intestinal problems, including Crohn's disease, diverticulitis, or spastic colon. Destructive habits like smoking and addictions are manifestations of depression, heartache, or unhappiness, which serve to create general body degradation.

Whatever organ holds the pain has some underlying weakness that attracts toxins. It's like a weak link in a chain—the result of a buildup of toxic energies in this organ in past lives (from karma, core issues, or past life trauma to a particular body area.

Western medicine treats coronary artery blockage syptomatically, not wholistically, with a bypass operation or a balloon angioplasty. Although both methods work in the short term, often within a year the repaired arteries end up in the same awful shape. The patients get to come back for a new round of operations.

What goes wrong?

The doctors operate on the *physical* heart without examining the *emotional* heart's pain, which manifests as heart disease. Blocked heart arteries are symptoms of blocked or unexpressed love; therefore, fixing the symptom does nothing for the underlying problem.

Dr. Dean Ornish, recognizing that underlying issues contributed to the disease, insisted that his heart bypass patients enroll in an intensive program that included a strict, low-fat diet, no smoking, meditation, yoga, and counseling for the patient and spouse. This regimen forced patients to confront unspoken or unexpressed feelings held within themselves and, thereby, release their heart's emotional blocks, so they wouldn't remanifest as physical blocks. Though the medical establishment was inclined to pooh-pooh Dr. Ornish's conclusions, they could not ignore his patients' dramatic results—little or no recurrence of the artery blockage.

Metaphor

Marlene's foot is another rather dramatic example of the process of releasing illness from the physical body. Until you confront the root cause of the disease, you cannot free yourself from it. You may disguise it, sublimate it, or treat the symptoms, but the cause still remains active and strong.When you focus on the disease's core, rather than symptoms, as is done with western medicine, you can deal with and even eradicate its roots.

The physical body is intimately connected to the emotional self–as you saw with childhood issues when we followed the body sensation to its emotional root. Because of some inherent weakness (i.e., wounding in a past life that affects a particular body area or organ), energy builds up, like food heated in a pressure cooker. Unless the pain is released in some way–venting emotions, stress reduction, meditation, exercise, counseling, etc.), it increases to such an intolerable level that it manifests as a physical disorder (the pressure cooker blowing its top).

With great reluctance, the medical profession has conceded that diseases like multiple sclerosis, asthma, and juvenile-onset diabetes have a major psychological component. Although they will not admit that these diseases might have a psychological root, they have concluded that emotions strongly affect the progress of these diseases.

Having seen too many instances where I could relate the disease or illness directly to the person's primary emotional issue, I believe all diseases have a psychological cause. By dealing with them on that level, you can effect a significant shift in the disease.

With any disease or illness, it is important to recognize the physical symptoms' *metaphoric* significance. By treating disease as a metaphor, you can find an underlying reason for getting it. A good book to consult about the correspondences between disease and emotions is Louise Hay's *Heal Your Body* (Hay House, Inc., 1988). She lists all kinds of diseases, the organs affected, and the psychological meaning of each problem.

If you examine the type of disease you have created, you will find you can trace its cause to your family situation, or behaviors or beliefs from your past. The origination point, however, is usually not in this life, but in one or several past lives.

Here are some examples:

Heart, chest, or lung problems indicate you have difficulty with love. Chest colds are your body's early warning about blocked or thwarted love, while heart attacks come on when the buildup of energy has become critical.

Breast cancer is not only disfiguring, but it represents the loss of nourishment. It is related to the difficulty of many women to give and get love and nurturance easily. Women with breast cancer have issues around being loved, being able to give love unconditionally, or their own worthiness.

Communication issues manifest in a whole range of ear, voice, and mouth problems.

Reasons For Disease

There are all kinds of reasons for taking on a disease, most of which directly relate to your present and past lives. When a disease develops in your body, it has a purpose and an intention, shaped by whatever lessons you have chosen to learn, and the childhood patterns you exhibit.

Here are some of the primary reasons for disease.

- To express repressed or intense emotions (usually related to your core issue)
- To relieve incredible emotional pressures.
- For personal emotional gain.
- Soul lessons for this lifetime.
- Karma.
- Predisposition (from past lives with the same problem).

Expressing Repressed Or Intense Emotions

By the age of three you have formed your patterns of survival. You know which behaviors will get your needs met—and which ones won't. If an emotion is deemed unacceptable (like anger) so it cannot be expressed, it remains locked in your body where it builds up pressure (much like a stream blocked by a dam). Eventually the pressure gets so intense that the dam must burst, and often does so in the form of sickness or disease.

In a systemic disease (for example, auto-immune diseases like rheumatic fever, lupus, chronic fatigue syndrome, etc.) the whole body participates in its collapse because the emotions connected to the initial wounding flood the whole body, reinforcing total body worthlessness.

One of the most intense of those disease-causing emotions is *shame*. In sexual abuse, the victim not only has a strong physical reaction in and around her vaginal area, she also experiences shame over the situation, worthlessness, and lowered self-esteem—all of which flood the whole body with toxins. A physical manifestation of that emotional turmoil might be juvenile-onset diabetes, or, later on, multiple sclerosis.

Incredible Emotional Pressures

When pressures in all aspects of your life become overwhelming, your body breaks down like the overburdened camel whose back was broken by a little straw. For example, divorce, the death of a loved one, loss of a job, or some other crisis that taps into core feelings of worthlessness can trigger outbursts or flareups of the disease process. For short-term stress, getting colds or flu is the body's way of releasing those pressures. However, if the stress continues long-term, the body takes more drastic action. The disease most commonly associated with such stress is cancer.

In fact, cancer cells are simply your own cells gone berserk; they are not alien invaders, like the HIV virus. Doctors can pump all kinds of toxic chemicals into the body in an attempt to kill the cancer cells, but—and it's a big *but*—they're only dealing with the symptoms, not the cause. Researchers don't know why and how you create cancer cells. Nor are they likely to find out, I believe, because they are looking for physical causes. Relentless emotional distress forces a cellular degeneration, which leads to cancer.

Stopping the disease process requires significant change—of job, home, relationship, scenery, diet, whatever is causing the stress, coupled with positive behaviors like exercise, good nutrition, relaxation or meditation, and a radical alteration in your attitudes, behaviors, beliefs, and feelings. In this high-pressure world, cancer provides an acceptable excuse for you to make changes without appearing as though you deliberately wanted to get off the high-pressure merry-go-round. Isn't there a better way of living than trying to kill yourself?

Curing cancer does not require nuking or excising the diseased organ, or poisoning the body with chemicals. It means seeking its cause and transforming it. The best tool for transforming illness into a healing life experience is by working with the physical body. By delving back into the past to find out when and why the body made the decision to take on the disease, you can begin to detoxify it.

Emotional Gain

What benefits do you derive from having a disease? Yes, having a disease has a payoff, no matter how negative it may first appear to you! How does your illness get you what you want—like attention and love?

You can use your disease to create some kind of emotional well-being and self-gratification, even though you may not realize it consciously. You may have heard it said that people get sick to get sympathy; it's their way to get emotional nurturance. In this case, the disease is generally a chronic condition, not an acute one. Emotional gain from sickness is fairly easy to spot; everyone ends up organizing his or her lives around the "patient." Alcoholics fall into this category.

Lessons

You come into each lifetime with certain lessons you have chosen to work on. Often a disease can give you invaluable help with issues like patience, gratitude, endurance, fortitude, and forgiveness. For a number of people, AIDS was such a lesson.

Why on earth would anyone want to endure such a debilitating dying experience? There are several answers. As we have moved into the Age of Aquarius with its new vibration, many people are taking the opportunity to shift their consciousness, sometimes quite dramatically. AIDS became a handy method for people to leave the planet if they so chose, or a way to work through a lot of karma in a short time. Some of them died angry and upset, while others refused to succumb to the disease and transformed themselves; dying became an enormously healing experience.

Karma

Do you wonder why some people are born with birth defects or develop illnesses such as cystic fibrosis, asthma, allergies, leukemia? I believe they are expressions of karma to atone for wrongs committed in other lives. Taking on an illness and living with the emotional and physical turmoil that it creates pays off a good chunk of your karmic debt, painful though it might he.

Predisposition

Some people have a genetic predisposition to different diseases, like breast or colon cancer, or diabetes. These predispositions merely indicate that a body weakness has built up over lifetimes, whether from uncompleted lifetimes, core issues, or karma.

Taking that concept one step further, I believe that you can choose not to activate the gene for a particular disease, if you work through the issues connected to it. *That*, of course, is the kicker. You have accumulated so much "stuff" from the emotional traumas of this life and past lives, that you need to devote an enormous effort to clean them up, in order to make a shift. People end up writing books explaining how they did it; and underlying every one of those stories is a single-minded dedication to heal themselves that many of us don't have. And that is what it takes: 24-hour-a-day dedication, but at the end of the process, your body is remarkably free of old toxic energies.

Anya had a severe problem with thrombophlebitis in her left leg. She discovered seven lives, one after another, in which her left leg was crushed, amputated, paralyzed, crippled, or rendered useless in some way. Because the original leg trauma was so intense, it left a mark on the soul that attracted more trauma to the now-energetically-sensitive leg in each subsequent lifetime. Healing her illness involved healing her leg in each of those past lives.

Core Issues

Now, or in a past life, your disease is affected by, or precipitated by, your core issue. For example, if you were neglected or abandoned by a parent in one life, and your issue is abandonment, you might manifest a debilitating illness in the next to get all the attention you need (you hope). If you were imprisoned in a small place, in a later life you would want to experience a lot of space, like being an explorer. Or if you got killed in a particularly brutal way you would want to create a safe environment.

Healing

To heal from a particular disease means disconnecting a belief system from your mind, releasing the emotions associated with the problem, and resolving the causal event that keeps generating the "stuff" that keeps the disease active. This means making a serious emotional commitment to processing your feelings, regaining your lost energies, embracing your Inner Child, and changing your past life scenarios—in other words, everything I've discussed in this book.

Let's look at some disease situations.

Marcy had breast cancer, and she dreaded having a mastectomy. To prevent that, she went into her a body and talked to her breasts, asking why they were becoming cancerous. The answer came back that they were unnurturing. The milk of love was not being given out. She had several children whom she alternately smothered and neglected, and a husband who was too busy with work for her. Her marriage was, in her words, "barren and lifeless," and so was her ability to give love.

I asked her to go back to the first time that she decided to create this family situation. The question led her into a past life where she was a young girl who was spurned by a man of higher station. When she married someone of her own class, she projected her bitterness at her rejection onto him and her children, so instead of giving love, she gave disdain. Along with past life and body-centered therapy for her, couples counseling helped them both work through their issues, and her breasts remained cancer-free.

Bob was dealing with an enlarged prostate and all that that implied about his sexuality and self-worth. The diagnosis left him an emotional and sexual wreck. As we worked together, he recognized that his prostate problem reflected the connection between his sexual image and his self-esteem. He had used his penis as a kind of weapon within his marriage. When he finally talked to his prostate (after much hemming and hawing), Bob learned that he had acted according to his father's beliefs about men's dominant role, repressing his own personal beliefs. By the time he began to accept the idea that there could be other ways of acting masculine that were not nearly so destructive to him, the prostate stopped growing, with no further development after several years without treatment.

These examples illustrate how nothing exists in a vacuum; a problem with one of your selves creates a resonance throughout the others because they all are interconnected and interdependent; therefore, treating the five parts of you as a group, not individually, promotes full body healing.

EXERCISES

Healing The Disease

There are a number of exercises in this book that can be applied and adapted for healing a disease. The childhood exercise (Chapter 8) and past life exercise (Chapter 15) are particularly useful to heal the emotional self and the soul. Auric cleanout in phobias (Chapter 16) remove disease energy. Finally, you can adapt the mind exercise in Chapter 6 or use the second exercise below on beliefs.

1. Lie comfortably, eyes closed. Soft music helps.

2. Invite your Higher Self to come with you to talk to your disease.

3. Imagine going down an elevator or escalator to the focal point of the disease.

4. Ask for your body's purpose in manifesting the illness. You may receive pictures, sounds, feelings or sensations. You will get some kind of message. If you don't see anything, just tune into a body sensation. Make it as strong as possible. (If you don't perceive anything, your mind doesn't want you to hear the message. It has an investment in keeping the status quo, no matter how destructive for the whole being.) Be persistent. Ask your Higher Self to help, if necessary. Your body does want to tell you what's wrong. After all, it's in pain and it would like the pain to stop, preferably without its death or maiming.

5. If you get a past life image, use the past life procedure in Chapter 15.

6. If your body part appears angry with you (you can tell), ask what it needs from you–whether it's acknowledgement, atonement, an apology, or commiseration. You'll be surprised at how often the organ in question will be more than delighted to get an apology. Mainly, it wants *acknowledgment* more than anything else for enduring all the stress of your life situation.

7. Ask your body whether it wants to be cured. *This is very important.* Part of your healing may actually mean suffering from this illness (this is a karmic issue).

8. To release karma, call on a karma angel.
   a. Ask it how much karma it will forgive–some or all of it.
   b. Then ask that the angel remove the karma from your diseased organ. You can picture it as a color. A good one is brown.

9. Ask your body, your Higher Self or an angel what the body needs to be healed. Perhaps it means doing Inner Child work (Chapter 8), past life work (Chapter 15), or forgiveness

(Chapter 18). Or just accepting what your guides and angels tell you.

10. Ask your organ what kind of a gift it would like to make it feel happier. Being bathed in a rainbow, receiving a gem, a song, etc., all of these may be acceptable–also a vacation, a new diet, icecream or chocolate, a change in a lifestyle, etc.

11. Ask your Higher Self and the pertinent organ for any remedies it might need which might be applied on the inner level or in actuality. (Marlene didn't have cherry bark on hand, but she visualized it on her foot.) The body might say, "I need a hug," or "Soak me in water," or "Take me away from here!" It will NOT say, "Cut me off," unless that leads to a greater good, like saving your life (and even in that case, it would have to be extremely serious).

12. Clean out the area.
    a. Flood the area with a color. Green is an all-purpose healing color, but gold or violet will work, as well.
    b. Breathe the sound *"aum"* into the area. This vibration helps break down emotional blockages, and breathe in the violet color of transformation.
    c. Put your hands on the area if you can get to it, or have friends do so, and breathe healing energy (gold or green) into it.

13. Visualize the area sparkling clean and healed.

14. Forgive yourself for hurting your organ, however unconsciously. Thank your organ for being willing to talk to you.

When you finish the process, do not assume that everything has been resolved. You have layers and layers to get rid of. Keep on recalling your healing visualization (step 12).

Releasing The Belief

In this exercise, you will be looking at the belief attached to the disease and disrupting it. (much of this exercise is similar to the exercise in Chapter 6).

1. Go into your sacred room, and invite your Higher Self to assist you.

2. Find your magic mirror on the wall and ask it to show you the body part that is hurting, in images, feelings, or words.

3. Ask that organ what belief is associated with its sickness. Often you will experience a feeling like shame or guilt or fear. Attached to that emotion, you may have a belief, often, "I'm worthless, " "I'm unlovable," "I'm no good."
4. Enhance that feeling so it fills your body, however uncomfortable it makes you. The more of it you feel, the more you will get rid of.
5. Imagine a large sunken bathtub filled with gold liquid. Climb into it. Sink all the way down so the liquid covers your head (you can breathe in gold). Imagine the gold liquid dissolving away the emotion you are feeling. A good image is of rock salt dissolving in water.
6. Say affirmations that counter that belief embedded in your organ. "I'm worthless" becomes "I'm worthwhile." "I'm not lovable" becomes "I'm lovable." "I'm no good" becomes "I'm good." This way you can begin to recalibrate your belief system at the cellular level. Always make your affirmations positive (do not use negative words in any of them).
7. Repeat the following affirmations. As you do, imagine the words being absorbed into the diseased part like silver glitter. This transforms the belief.
   a. "I love [name the affected organ]."
   b. "I forgive myself. I forgive [name the affected organ]." .
8. If more emotion comes up, repeat steps 4, 5, and 6.

CHAPTER 18
RESPONSIBILITY

For a number of years, it has become normal to blame our parents for our messy lives: "It's not my fault that I'm the way I am," we proclaim. "My mother and my father screwed up my life." In fact, our parents did make mistakes raising us—mostly unintentionally (most of them were "good enough parents", which is all we can expect of anyone), but some parents were really horrible, and the children they produced are too often in our prison system.

Until recently, people muddled through their lives in spite of being emotional cripples, passing on to their children dysfunctions that have been in their families since, probably, Adam and Eve. Now, we publicly dissect in great detail behaviors once thought acceptable (like drinking) or hidden (sexual abuse), on public forums of all sorts. We are finding the courage to release our old dysfunctional patterns and move toward healing. One of those critically important healing processes involves blaming our abusers.

Once your Inner Child accepts that he or she was an innocent victim of childhood trauma—as far as they're concerned, they endured serious abuse— they need to vent their once-impotent rage on their abusers. Releasing this pent-up fury is not only justifiable, but it is *essential* for the Child's healing and self-empowerment. That might mean pounding pillows in therapy, up to actually suing a parent in court.

Who's really to blame?

There's no question that your parents (and their ancestors) were at fault for perpetuating certain bad behaviors. I'm sure you can point to many examples from your life to buttress your claims against your parents. But let's look at this issue from a different perspective—by asking why you put yourself into that abusive situation in the first place.

"Me!?" you object. "I didn't choose that abuse!"

In point of fact, you probably did. (That would be karma.)

Unlike your Child, *you*, the adult, are capable of seeing your life in a larger perspective—and there is one. Your Higher Self chose your family, not only for the lessons you needed to learn, but also to resolve the karma that provoked the abuse in the first place. This maybe difficult for you to believe, never mind, accept. Who wants to acknowledge that they chose to be born into a sexually, emotionally, or physically abusive family? Nevertheless, your Higher Self didn't just choose your parents randomly; it found a family situation that would provide the best karmic lesson for you in this lifetime.

When you were a child, you had no capacity or ability to see the larger picture, but the adult can perceive, and understand, the full implications of your abuse. You're not an innocent, like it or not. You've been around the block, so to speak, for many lifetimes, creating karma, paying it back, making mistakes and learning lessons. If your father was a sexual abuser, chances are that you did the same thing to him in another lifetime. You set up this whole experience—not to mortify yourself or provide your Child with a wretched experience. Although you don't have to like what happened to your Child, it was part of your karmic lesson.

On the other hand, telling your Child to accept the abuse and forgive her parents because of what you did in a previous life is plain foolish. She or he simply hasn't got the emotional capacity to understand, nor the willingness. All she is aware of is the pain. Also, explaining about atonement or forgiveness merely prevents her from expressing her feelings, and creates even more anger inside her.

RESPONSIBILITY

In the 1970s and '80s, the personal growth gurus claimed (rightly) that we were responsible for every thing that happened in our lives, but they said it in such a judgmental way that made many of us feel wrong if we didn't admit our responsibility for the situation and change it *immediately*. They didn't understand human behavior and the role shame or guilt plays in preventing us from facing our issues.

Change is a step-by-step process, most easily accomplished in a safe, loving environment, not in an accusatory or hostile one. Unfortunately, most of us tend to be highly judgmental about ourselves and others, which breeds self-guilt and blame, so that any change we undertake is painful, at best.

Since you are the only one who can make changes in your life, forcing you to look at something with little preparation and less emotional support doesn't foster positive change and healing; instead it generates more resistance. It takes time, effort, and faith in your ability to make amends to face your responsibility.

Only when you're emotionally and spiritually ready can you acknowledge that you might indeed have a karmic connection with the parents you chose. That's when you say, "What can I do to heal this experience?"

Continuing to blame your parents for your present life keeps you stuck where you are (and safe). Laying on blame like a thick blanket is easy, expedient–and non-productive in the long run. It provides short-term satisfaction, but ultimately accomplishes little.

Conversely, you can decide that the cause of this situation stems from your behavior in another lifetime, and proceed to blame yourself for having done all those terrible deeds then that created this karma. You have now become a martyr. That's just as counterproductive–and equally invalid–as blaming others. It's important to recognize your responsibility in your past, but flagellating yourself impedes the resolution of your present life issues and abuse.

In a previous chapter, I mentioned Aliena, who in her past lifetime had been horribly vicious to her spouse, and was now paying the price in her present deeply unhappy marriage. She remained stuck until she recognized her responsibility for paying off past life karma with her husband. Once she did that, she effectively completed the karma and divorced the creep.

You can come to terms with your present life by recognizing: 1) your abuse was karma you've *chosen* to pay and 2) your Child needs to be allowed to heal in appropriate ways, including expressing his or her rage at their current abusers for as long as he or she needs.

Your Inner Child knows instinctively that it is necessary to release the rage she or he carries, and transforming the abuse, incident by incident. That helps release those trapped toxins from both your emotional and physical bodies. Then, as the rage, hostility, or sadness get expressed– and released, space opens inside you, which provides more clarity and perspective–until you can acknowledge that you had a share in creating your karma as well.

That's one reason it is so important to allow the angels to flood you with love over and over again, to release that buried rage from your very cells. Once removed, it *never comes back.*

After all that, your next step is to express any other feelings that might be related to this situation. Only then can you open your heart to true forgiveness, in whatever form that takes.

FORGIVENESS

You might have heard that you must forgive everyone and everything to evolve. That's a great concept, but true forgiveness only happens after cleaning out your pent-up rage. Many adults have told me how they forgave their parents, but when I asked their Inner Children, I found that they had *no* intention of forgiving the parents until their rage and fury had been expressed and transformed.

You will not burn in hell if you do not forgive your abuser, but your evolution will be harder if you don't. It's like a sack of boulders you're dragging behind you. You can feel self-righteous in holding on to the abuse like a precious possession: "They destroyed my life. Now I'm going to suffer forever. I'll show them!" (Martyrdom like that gets tiresome after a while.) It takes a lot of effort to hold on to blame, and it just perpetuates your karma. Part of the work of forgiveness is letting yourself experience joy. It's much easier to flagellate yourself into sinlessness than enjoy yourself.

Overly-eager forgiveness disregards the Inner Child's true feelings of rage, no matter how much you the adult might like to get past them. It takes time for the Child to release those feelings, particularly, sexual abuse), and in many cases, that may not occur for a long time, maybe not even in this lifetime.

When you are ready you can take the next step in your healing process—forgiving the abuser. By talking about forgiving your parents (even if you reject the idea), you begin the process of reclaiming yourself from your own victimhood. Yet it *cannot be done before it is time.* That means you can't rush into forgiveness either.

Forgiveness doesn't happen overnight; it takes years, and comes with spiritual maturity. You can consider the process of forgiveness as a mortgage on your house—the first few years you're only paying interest, but when you start paying off the principal (i.e., cleaning away cartloads of rage and blame), your equity (forgiveness) starts rising precipitately. As your anger level drops, your forgiveness level rises.

You won't feel much forgiveness at first, or even for a long time. It helps if, at the end of any process, you ask yourself for as much "forgiveness toward your abuser as you are willing to allow at this time. If you can't even ask that question, don't give up hope. It means that you still have got a lot of rage to clear away. Or you might dislodge just one micron of forgiveness, but it's one micron more than before.

Forgiveness might not happen in this lifetime–but it must be done, sooner or later, until one day you look at your parents, your childhood, and your life, and feel love and acceptance untainted by judgment or anger. Until that time, remember that you are working on yourself, and that's all-important.

EXCERCISE

You can do this exercise over and over again until you reach a point of completion with yourself or another person.

1. Sit in a quiet spot with a piece of paper and a pen. Close your eyes. Clean out your aura and bring yourself into present time. (Don't keep parts of yourself stuck in the past during this exercise. It's intense enough as it is.)

2. Invite your Higher Self to participate with you. You need its help! Imagine yourself in a room with a door.

3. Imagine someone you want to forgive. If you do not want to see the person because the sight of them will get you very upset, keep them behind a door. Otherwise, let them sit beside the door–away from you.

4. Imagine forgiveness as a barrel of blue water.

5. Ask yourself how much forgiveness you have toward this person.

6. Even asking yourself the question can trigger enormous rage. That's perfectly acceptable. Imagine that rage as dark red liquid inside another barrel. (You have two barrels–forgiveness and rage.)

7. Ask your Higher Self to remove from the rage barrel as much rage toward that person as you are willing to release at this time. That might mean a dropper, a cup, a bucket, or nothing at all. Pour that rage onto the earth for recycling.

8. Now repeat Step 5. You might find that you are ready to give a tiny amount of forgiveness. If you don't know how much, ask your Higher Self to take out as much forgiveness as you are willing to give. There is no penalty for not giving out any forgiveness.

9. Pass that cup of forgiveness to the person you're angry at. As you continue to repeat the exercise, over time, you will release more rage and send out more forgiveness.

10. Forgiveness also applies to you as well. Take as much forgiveness toward yourself as you can accept. Many times, it is difficult for you to forgive yourself, long after your atonement is over.

11. Let the forgiveness liquid flow through you.

12. You can repeat Step 10 with your Higher Self or an angel. It's instructive to realize that other beings love and forgive you much more than you allow yourself to be loved.

CHAPTER 19
LIFE PURPOSE AND YOUR DIVINE BLUEPRINT

When you take on too much responsibility, or remain in denial, or blame yourself far beyond what is right for yourself, or refuse to acknowledge your part of the problem for yourself and your world, or feel at the mercy of someone else or your emotions, you are out of balance. Balance is a result of accepting your share of the personal responsibility–and *no more*.

But finding and knowing what is balance, and when you are in balance is very tricky. Like schizophrenics who get off their medicine, thinking they're fine until they are taken to the hospital, most of us do not recognize when we are out of balance. Looking back in hindsight, we can say, "It's clear my life was a mess and I made very stupid decisions, but I couldn't see the forest for the trees." Being in balance helps you make clear, positive decisions about your life; it also indicates that you are in alignment with your Higher Self, and your Life Purpose.

I've talked about your Life Purpose in the first chapter. It is what your Higher Self has chosen as your major task for this lifetime. But more than that, it is yourself feeling complete from the inside out. It brings healing and balance to every part of your life.

It's not necessary that your Life Purpose fall into a particular classification (as if there were only ten possible options, and if you're not doing one of those ten, you're a failure), *as long as you do it.* Here are some examples: running a ranch to preserve nature; teaching spirituality, though not from an obvious "spiritual" perspective; creating nonprofits for worthy causes. Those are only a minuscule fraction of the possible spiritual Life Purposes. And then there are those Life Purposes that are more in the world–as leaders, inventors, thinkers (like Gandhi or Martin Luther King).

A fulfilled Life Purpose enhances the quality of life of the practitioner and the people around him or her. Those people who gain wealth, power, or prestige by stepping on others or raping the earth are not manifesting a Life Purpose. Doing so is out of balance and against your Life Purpose—and will come back to bite you sometime later.

Some people sense their Life Purpose, but its message is distorted by their mental screens. Their imperfect vision, if it is imposed on others, can cause all sorts of damage. Typical comments from them are, "I have the answer, and you can get it only from me." Or, "I see *the Truth*, and you must follow me to improve your life." Instead of guiding people into healing or new spiritual perspectives, they become destructive by limiting and preventing people from manifesting their own Life Purpose. Organized religion is rife with such people. (Here's a tip: Anything with the word "organized" means someone has an agenda that they are imposing on others, though many of these followers feel safe and protected—until the moment they start questioning any of the tenets of that religion.)

Parents also put pressure on their children to follow their plan, which often is counter to their children's Life Purpose. That's why many of these children come to me, trying to undo those programs their parents instilled in them.

The single most important goal in your personal work is to clear away the baggage of the past in order to fulfil your Life Purpose. When you recognize that your life is not working, that is when you are more likely to work to create deep, lasting change. Psychological and spiritual disciplines can clear childhood issues and mental screens, and help you become more connected to your Higher Self. Once that happens, you are more likely to find the direction that leads to your Life Purpose, so that you are in alignment with the universe and in balance with yourself.

At first, you may not be able to understand or even conceive of your Life Purpose. Gradually, it becomes clearer and clearer, until doing it feels completely natural and right. Then you are in balance. I like to describe it as the gold level. You are connected to your Higher Self, to the angels, to Source, and in alignment with all of your bodies. You have boundless energy and love for the people around you. You know you are in exactly the right place doing the right thing.

DIVINE BLUEPRINT

Your Life Purpose is you doing what you need to manifest your highest level, while your Divine Blueprint holds your Life Purpose. It is the plan for who and what you are, and was given to your Higher Self before your birth. You might call it your "potential" for perfection, that sense of greatness of who you can be. But it got disconnected from your earthly consciousness early in life.

The Divine Blueprint has all of your wisdom and skill to manifest your Life Purpose. When you bring the Divine Blueprint into your body, it becomes much easier to come into balance and find and express your Life Purpose.

The first time you bring your Divine Blueprint into your body, your cells wake up, your spirit starts to sing, and all those parts of you realign themselves into the highest vibration possible.

EXERCISE

Aligning with your Divine Blueprint

1. Find a quiet spot. Clean out your aura and bring yourself into present time.
2. Call in your Higher Self. You cannot do this exercise without your Higher Self. By this time you should have a good relationship with her/him.
3. Stand up. You are going to take off your energy field (aura).
4. Unzip your aura. Reach up with your hand to grasp the zipper above your head, and unzip the aura from the top of your head to your feet. Climb out of it, and let it sit on the ground. We'll get back to it in a little bit.
5. Ask your Higher Self to hand you you Divine Blueprint. It looks like a bod suit of iridescent energy that is flexible and light.

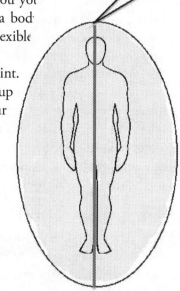

6. Climb into your Divine Blueprint. Put it over your feet. Pull it up your legs, over your hips, up your torso. Put your hands and arms inside and pull it up over your shoulders. Then put it over your head and face.
7. Now let it sink into your body, into your cells, your molecules, your DNA. Wherever it goes, it sparkles.
8. Because it is a Divine Blueprint, it vibrates at a divine level. As

you breathe in and out slowly (count of 6 for inhale and 6 for exhale, ten times), you are allowing the blueprint to release anything that does not vibrate at the divine level–from your DNA, all the way up to your organs and your selves. You don't have to do anything; all you have to do is breathe.

9. Pick up your aura. Shake it as if you were shaking out a rug.
10. Climb back into your aura and zip it up.

CHAPTER 20
HEALING YOUR PAST

I have long recognized that we have chosen to come to this planet for a larger purpose than to merely survive year after year. We have come here to fulfill our life purpose, which may be specific to this lifetime or part of a much larger pattern that extends through many lifetimes. Yet underlying this life purpose is something even more profound–the self-evolution of our soul, and the evolution of humanity, in its many forms.

We all left the Godhead on our great journey of learning, innocent as newborns. With the first decision we made, we lost our innocence, never to be reclaimed–but that was the purpose of our journey. If it were, we would have remained attached to the Godhead, as angels.

We chose that arduous and tortuous route toward transcendence, toward reintegration with Source, to become wise beings. Innocence is charming but limiting; wisdom creates total harmony with the will of the Godhead, tempered with the experience of self and the manifestation of life purpose. During our long, long journey of life, we have made wonderful connections, incredible mistakes, joyful creations, great blunders–all necessary elements of any evolutionary process.

This is the journey I have undertaken, along with many others. Some of us recognized that they have been on this path forever, while others are just now awakening to the call of self-transformation. Many of us feel that we are fighting to transform while drowning in a sea of unwanted and limiting patterns, needs, emotions, and fears that have governed us from our earliest childhoods. How can we overcome them on our way to the manifestation of our life purpose and self-evolution? I felt an enormous frustration at being trapped in those old patterns and fears. I wanted to break away and become a new person–and yet, I was scared of what I would become.

When I decided to write this book, I imagined it as a healing process for me, as well as a manual that others might find useful. At the time, I wanted to focus on the psychological issues, but as the book evolved, I realized that I was expressing part of my own spiritual journey through my writing.

I began with a desire to put the past to rest, to get rid of the attitudes, patterns, and behaviors that had haunted me like the luggage from hell for most of my life. I thought that meant going back to my childhood and making the changes that would release those patterns, but I found that that was only part of the process.

I needed to transmute those feelings, needs, and fears into something positive that could help me evolve. I imagined it, not like only dropping the battered luggage, but allowing it to be recycled—with my blessing and good wishes.

I like to call it "evolving." It means focusing not on the past but on the future—moving toward a goal, however amorphous it might appear at the present, that defines and expresses my life purpose.

I can guarantee you that our Life Purpose does not mean regurgitating our childhood issues until doomsday. Healing from our childhood is a necessary step in order to move toward fulfilling our life purpose, but not the major one. We cannot evolve unless we stop floundering around in our childhood, and call a halt to all that inner angst. By being stuck there, we lose sight of our own inner divinity, our own inner wisdom, and our chosen path. We need to begin to direct ourselves and our lives toward a new vision—the vision of what we want to be, rather than where we have been. I'm saying all this, not from a perspective of lofty detachment, but because I have spent a long time in the trenches of childhood pain and unhappiness.

The most important thing I learned was that if I chose to stay stuck in the past, it would be difficult for me to create a healing, loving, or wise present or future. I didn't want to limit myself because of my childhood fears, patterns, and inertia (even though it was safer being the way I had been).

When I started my work, I didn't have any idea about life purposes. I only knew that what I was doing wasn't working for me, and I let my Higher Self guide me. In my work as a psychic, I found that chunks and pieces of my confusion disappeared until I gradually found myself seeing a clearer picture of my life and its purpose.

Because of that, I began to guide other people into their own inner world to release their blocks and fears. Since I wanted to be sure my work was safe and impeccable, I became a transpersonal psychotherapist, working to bridge the spiritual with the psychological. The results have been quite positive and healing for my clients—and myself—and the result is this book (and others I have written that continue the theme of transformation). You have tools and techniques that will help you release the tyranny of the past in its many forms, and let you embrace your life purpose, whatever that is.

The question you might ask is "Can you do any of these exercises yourself?" and the answer is "Nobody else can." You could have a friend read the steps, or record them, and stop the recording while you process, but the fact is that only you can do what needs to be done. It takes only willingness and openness to facilitate your healing.

The process is ongoing and multilayered. It's like a spiral. Once you work on an issue and think you've cleared it, it recurs later on, at a deeper level, from this life, and from past lives. That's why the process is so relentless and interminable. We're doing double duty—not only do we work to heal this life, but all the earlier lives as well. The process takes time, and yet we do create significant change. That's the only constant in our lives.

One of the most important things to remember is that with each process, you are supporting your self—the creation, breaking free of the limiting behaviors, beliefs, needs, and negative emotions that have run your life so far. That means you will find yourself making different choices about your lifestyle, your friends, family, work situations—all based on your life purpose, rather than inner emotional needs. Transformation is creating the possibility for unlimited expansion of being.

We *can* do it—if we remember that we are not doing this alone; we are in partnership with our Higher Self, the Godhead, angels, and with whomever we want to bring in to help us. It is a joint effort—it does not need to be drudgery.

I've addressed the problems you might encounter as you are transforming yourself, but I haven't mentioned what you will transform yourself into. I don't know that answer. Personally, I hope you will be a wonderful, magnetic being of light.

I imagine that you will be, as you keep transforming, is more aware psychically and spiritually of yourself and others. There is much I haven't said about spiritual transformation and awareness; that is beyond the scope of this book.

The hallmark of spiritual awakening is the boundless urge for transformation, whether it manifests as simply the desire for change, or a restlessness to step beyond ourselves. Eventually, it comes down to moving into lightness of being—what has been called "walking lightly on the earth." That doesn't mean we have to lose weight; it means that our bodies become lighter because they are no longer filled with blocks, alien energies, or stuck in places that dragged us down.

We chose to be here on this planet, at this time in history, not because we wanted to leave, but because we wanted to resolve karma—for ourselves, our family groups, the country, and the planet. We wanted to do it now, so that at the end of this lifetime, those of us who are ready can choose your movement toward Ascension. We appear normal, but inside we are filled with joy—perhaps not every day of our lives, but for a considerable number of them.